IN THE COMPANY OF THE QURAN

IN THE COMPANY OF THE QURAN

AN EXPLANATION OF SURAH MARYAM

BY **FURHAN ZUBAIRI**

Followed by an Appendix on the Structure and Cohesion of Surah Maryam by **Munir Eltal**

Printed in the United States of America

First Publishing, 2021

ISBN: 9798478379278

Cover design, layout, and typesetting: Mohammad Bibi
Typeset in Lato, Nassim, and KFGQPC Uthmanic Script HAFS
Arabic Symbols: KFGQPC Arabic Symbols 01

Dedicated to my wife Fatima Rangoonwala whose tireless efforts allow me to dedicate my time to reading and writing.

Contents

INTRODUCTION

INTRODUCTION TO SŪRAH MARYAM

EXPLANATION OF SŪRAH MARYAM

The Story of Zakariyyā ﷵ

The Story of Yaḥyā ﷵ

The Other Prophets & Messengers عليهم السلام

Those Who Came After Them

Everything Belongs to Allah ﷻ

Allah ﷻ Will Raise the Dead & Everyone Will Witness Hellfire

Allah ﷻ Addresses Those Who Oppose The Messenger ﷺ & His Followers ﷺ

STRUCTURE & COHESION OF SŪRAH MARYAM

BIBLIOGRAPHY

Transliteration & Pronunciation Key

Arabic Letter	Transliteration	Sound
ء	ʾ	A slight catch in the breath, cutting slightly short the preceding syllable.
ا	*ā*	An elongated *a* as in *cat*.
ب	*b*	As in *best*.
ت	*t*	As in *ten*.
ث	*th*	As in *thin*.
ج	*j*	As in *jewel*.
ح	*ḥ*	Tensely breathed *h* sound made by dropping tongue into back of throat, forcing the air out.
خ	*kh*	Pronounced like the *ch* in Scottish *loch*, made by touching back of tongue to roof of mouth and forcing air out.
د	*d*	As in *depth*.
ذ	*dh*	A thicker *th* sound as in *the*.
ر	*r*	A rolled *r*, similar to Spanish.
ز	*z*	As in *zest*.
س	*s*	As in *seen*.
ش	*sh*	As in *sheer*.
ص	*ṣ*	A heavy *s* pronounced far back in the mouth with the mouth hollowed to produce full sound.
ض	*ḍ*	A heavy *d/dh* pronounced far back in the mouth with the mouth hollowed to produce a full sound.
ط	*ṭ*	A heavy *t* pronounced far back in the mouth with the mouth hollowed to produce a full sound.
ظ	*ẓ*	A heavy *dh* pronounced far back in the mouth with the mouth hollowed to produce a full sound.
ع	ʿ	A guttural sound pronouned narrowing the throat.
غ	*gh*	Pronounced like a throaty French *r* with the mouth hallowed.
ف	*f*	As in *feel*.
ق	*q*	A guttural *q* sound made from the back of the throat with the mouth hallowed.
ك	*k*	As in *kit*.
ل	*l*	As in *lip*.
م	*m*	As in *melt*.
ن	*n*	As in *nest*.
ه	*h*	As in *hen*.

و	*w* (at the beg. of syllable)	As in *west.*
	ū (in the middle of syllable)	An elongated *oo* sound, as in *boo.*
ي	*y* (at beg. of syllable)	As in *yes.*
	ī (in the middle of syllable)	An elongated *ee* sound, as in *seen.*

سُبْحَانَهُ وَتَعَالَىٰ Used following the mention of Allah, God, translated as, "Glorified and Exalted be He."

صَلَّى ٱللَّهُ عَلَيْهِ وَسَلَّمَ Used following the mention of the Prophet Muḥammad, translated as, "May God honor and protect him."

عَلَيْهِ ٱلسَّلَامُ Used following the mention of any other prophet or Gabriel, translated as, "May God's protection be upon him."

رَضِيَ ٱللَّهُ عَنْهُمْ Used following the mention of the Prophet Muḥammad's Companions, translated as, "May God be pleased with them."

رَضِيَ ٱللَّهُ عَنْهُ Used following the mention of a male Companion of the Prophet Muḥammad, translated as, "May God be pleased with him."

رَضِيَ ٱللَّهُ عَنْهَا Used following the mention of a female Companion of the Prophet Muḥammad, translated as, "May God be pleased with her."

رَضِيَ ٱللَّهُ عَنْهُمَا Used following the mention of two Companions of the Prophet Muḥammad, translated as, "May God be pleased with them both."

رَحِمَهُمُ ٱللَّهُ Used following the mention of the major scholars of Islam, translated as, "May God have mercy on them."

رَحِمَهُ ٱللَّهُ Used following the mention of a major scholar of Islam, translated as, "May God have mercy on him."

INTRODUCTION

بسم الله الرحمن الرحيم

In the Name of Allah, the Most Merciful, the Very Merciful. All thanks and praise are due to Allah ﷻ, the Lord of the worlds, and may His blessings and protection be upon His last and final messenger, Muḥammad ﷺ, his family, his companions, and those who follow them until the end of times.

It truly is a great blessing and favor of Allah ﷻ that He has granted me both the opportunity and ability to study, explore, and pen a few pages about the meanings of His blessed and divine words. I'm truly grateful and humbled for this opportunity. May Allah ﷻ accept this effort, place it on my scale of good deeds, and allow me to continue being a student of the Quran.

In the last volume, I was able to complete an explanation of Sūrah al-Kahf based on a number of classical and contemporary works of Tafsīr. God willing, in this volume we'll be exploring the meanings, lessons, and reminders of Sūrah Maryam. Tafsīr is an extremely noble and virtuous discipline. The reason why it's so noble and virtuous is because it's the study of the divine speech of Allah ﷻ. As mentioned in a ḥadīth, the superiority of the speech of Allah ﷻ over all other speech is like the superiority of Allah ﷻ Himself over all of His creation. There's nothing more beneficial and virtuous than studying the Quran. By doing so we'll be counted amongst the best of people. As the Prophet ﷺ said, "The best amongst you are those who learn the Quran and teach it."[1]

All of us need to build a stronger relationship with the Quran. The Quran is full of wisdom and guidance in every single verse and word. It's our re-

1 Bukhārī, *k. faḍā'il al-Quran, b. khayrukum man taʿllama al-quran wa ʿallama*, 5027

sponsibility to seek that guidance, understand it, contextualize it, and more importantly act upon it. Tafsīr is such a unique discipline that it brings together all of the other Islamic sciences. While exploring a Sūrah, a person comes across discussions regarding Arabic grammar and morphology, rhetoric, ḥādīth, fiqh, sīrah and all other topics that are studied and discussed as part of the Islamic Sciences. One scholar described the Quran as an ocean that has no shore. The more we study the Quran, the stronger our relationship with it will become. We'll become more and more attached to it and will be drawn into its beauty and wonder. The deeper a person gets into tafsīr and studying, the more engaged and interested they become. They also recognize how little they truly know. Studying the Quran helps nurture and develop humility. That's the nature of true knowledge. The more we learn, the more we recognize how much we don't know. May Allah ﷻ allow us all to be sincere and committed students of the Quran.

This is the second volume in a series that I'm entitling *In the Company of the Quran*. The long-term goal is to produce and publish an original explanation of the entire Quran in English based on classical and contemporary sources, God willing. May Allah ﷻ grant success to this project, accept it, and make it a means of connecting people to the Quran.

I would like to thank all of those individuals who provided suggestions, comments, improvements and took the time out of their busy schedules to edit this short work. May Allah ﷻ reward our IOK Seminary student Munir Eltal and and Seminary graduate Mudassir Mayet, continue to bless them, and increase them in knowledge. I would also like to thank Sr. Sara Bokker and my wife, Fatima Rangoonwala, for providing beneficial suggestions and editing the work.

INTRODUCTION TO SURAH MARYAM

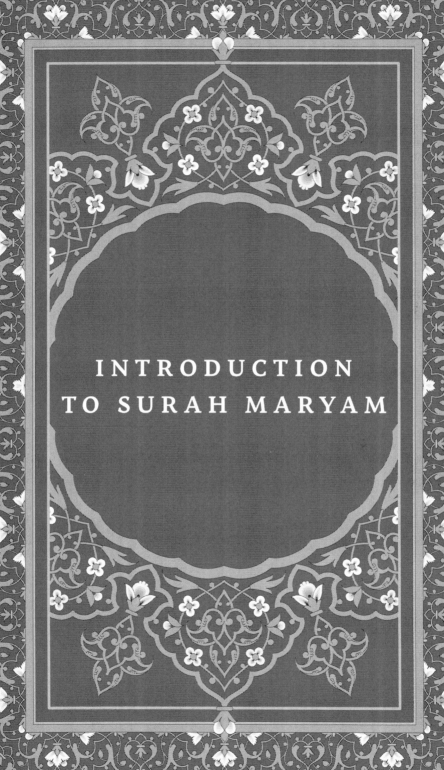

Sūrah Maryam is the 19th Sūrah in the Quran. It is a relatively long Makkan Sūrah made up of 98 verses. Some commentators mention that it's the 44th Sūrah to be revealed, after Sūrah al-Fāṭir and before Sūrah ṬāHā. It has been given the name Maryam because Allah ﷻ mentions the story of Maryam ؏ and her family and how she miraculously gave birth to ʿIsā ؏ at the beginning of the Sūrah. Just like other Makkan revelation, it deals with the most fundamental aspects of our faith. It talks about the existence and oneness of Allah ﷻ, prophethood, resurrection, and recompense.

The Sūrah is made up of a series of unique stories filled with guidance and lessons that are meant as reminders. One of the main themes of this Sūrah is the infinite, limitless, all-encompassing, and divine mercy of Allah ﷻ. Mercy, or raḥmah, has been mentioned over 16 times in this beautiful and powerful Sūrah. We'll find the words of grace, compassion, and their synonyms frequently mentioned throughout the Sūrah, together with Allah's attributes of beneficence and mercy. We can say that one of the objectives of the Sūrah is to establish and affirm the attribute of mercy for Allah ﷻ. That's why all of the stories mentioned also have to do with Allah's infinite mercy.

Another objective of the sūrah is to remind us of our relationship with Allah ﷻ; the concept of al-ʿUbūdiyyah. There are also several scenes and references to life after death and the Day of Judgment. These are the three major themes or ideas of this sūrah; the concepts of raḥmah (mercy), ʿubūdiyyah (servitude), and qiyāmah (life after death).

The Sūrah can be divided into eight sections:

1. Verses 1-15: The sūrah starts with the story of Zakariyyā ﷺ and how he was given the gift of a child at a very old age, which was something strange and out of the ordinary.
2. Verses 16-40: Allah ﷻ mentions the story of Maryam ﷺ and the miraculous birth of ʿIsā ﷺ without a father and how her community responded to her.
3. Verses 41-50: Allah ﷻ briefly mentions an episode from the life of Ibrāhīm ﷺ, specifically the conversation he had with his father regarding idol worship. This is followed by a brief mention of a series of other Prophets.
4. Verses 51-58: Allah ﷻ briefly mentions Mūsā and Hārūn ﷺ, Ismāʿīl ﷺ, and Idrīs ﷺ to show that the essence of the message of all Prophets was the same.
5. Verses 59-65: In these verses, Allah ﷻ compares and contrasts the previous generations with the current ones in terms of belief and actions.
6. Verses 66-72: Allah ﷻ addresses the Polytheists rejecting their false claims regarding life after death and judgment.
7. Verses 73-87: Allah ﷻ continues to address the Polytheists and warns them regarding their attitude towards belief in Allah ﷻ and His messengers. He ﷻ also mentions the great difference between the resurrection of a believer and the resurrection of a non-believer.
8. Verses 88-98: In these verses, there is a severe warning to those who claim that Allah ﷻ has taken a child. The verses also express that Allah ﷻ is pleased with the believers and mention that one of the objectives of the Quran is to give glad tidings to the believers and to warn the non-believers.

BACKGROUND

From various narrations, we learn that this Sūrah was revealed near the end of the fourth year of Prophethood. This was an extremely difficult time for the Muslims. The Quraysh were frustrated with their inability to stop the message of Islam from spreading and they became ruthless and more audacious in their persecution of the growing minority Muslim community. They resorted to any method of torture they could think of; beating, starving, and harassing. When the persecution became so severe that it was difficult for the Muslims to bear, the Prophet ﷺ gave permission to a group of Companions to migrate to Abyssinia, "for in it dwells a king in whose presence no one is harmed."[2] Ten men and four women migrated secretly in the fifth year of Prophethood. After a few months, a larger group of 83 men and eighteen women migrated as well. This migration added more fuel to the fire, enraging the leaders of Quraysh.

Umm Salamah ؓ narrated, "When we stopped to reside in the land of Abyssinia we lived alongside the best of neighbors, al-Najāshī. We practiced our religion safely, worshipped Allah ﷻ without harm, and didn't hear anything we disliked. When news of our situation reached the Quraysh they started to plot against us…" They decided to send two delegates to persuade al-Najāshī to send the Companions back by offering him and his ministers wealth and gifts. The plan was to go to each minister with gifts and turn them against the Muslims. They went to each minister with gifts and said, "Verily, foolish youth from among us have come to the country of your king; they have abandoned the religion of their people and have not embraced your religion. Rather, they have come with a new religion that neither of us knows. The noblemen of their people, from their fathers and uncles, have sent us to the king asking that he send them back. When we speak to the king regarding their situation, advise him to surrender them to us and to not speak to them…" They essentially bribed the ministers and they easily agreed.

Then they went to the king, offered him gifts, and said the same thing. The ministers tried to convince him as well. al-Najāshī became angry with them and said, "No, by Allah ﷻ, I will not surrender them to these two and I don't fear the plotting of a people who have become my neighbors, have settled down in my country, and have chosen me (to grant them refuge) over every other person. I will not do so until I summon them and speak to them. If they are as these two say, I will give them up, but if they aren't, then I will protect them from these two and continue to be a good neighbor to them as long as they are good neighbors to me."[3]

al-Najāshī then summoned the Prophet's Companions. When his mes-

---

2   al-Bayhaqī, *al-Sunan al-Kubrā*, 9:16 #177734

3   Ḥanbal, *Musnad*, 1740

senger informed the Prophet's Companions that they were to appear before the king, they gathered together to discuss what they should do. One of them asked, "What will you say to the person (al-Najāshī) when you go to him?" They all agreed on what they would say to him, "By Allah, we will say what our Prophet ﷺ taught us and commanded us with, regardless of the consequences." Meanwhile, al-Najāshī called for his priests, who gathered around him with their scrolls spread out before them. When the Muslims arrived, al-Najāshī began by asking them, "What is this religion for which you have parted from your people? You have not entered into the fold of my religion, nor the religion of any person from these nations."

Umm Salamah ﵂ narrated, "The person among us who spoke to him was Jaʿfar ibn abī Ṭālib ﵁ who then said, 'O king, we were an ignorant people: we worshipped idols, we would eat from the flesh of dead animals, we would perform lewd acts, we would cut off family ties, and we would be bad neighbors; the strong among us would eat from the weak. We remained upon that state until Allah ﷻ sent us a Messenger, whose lineage, truthfulness, trustworthiness, and chastity we already knew. He invited us to Allah ﷻ - to believe in His oneness and to worship Him; to abandon all that we and our fathers worshipped besides Allah ﷻ, in terms of stones and idols. He ﷺ commanded us to speak truthfully, to fulfill the trust, to join ties of family relations, to be good to our neighbors, and to refrain from forbidden deeds, and from shedding blood. And he ﷺ forbade us from lewd acts, from uttering falsehood, from wrongfully eating the wealth of an orphan, and from falsely accusing chaste women of wrongdoing. And he ﷺ ordered us to worship Allah ﷻ alone and to not associate any partners with Him in worship; and he ﷺ commanded us to pray, to give zakāh, and to fast.' He enumerated for al-Najāshī the teachings of Islam. He said, 'And we believe him and have faith in him. We follow him in what he came with. And so we worship Allah ﷻ alone, without associating any partners with Him in worship. We deem forbidden that which he has made forbidden for us, and we deem lawful that which he made permissible for us. Our people then transgressed against us and tortured us. They tried to force us to abandon our religion and to return from the worship of Allah ﷻ to the worship of idols; they tried to make us deem lawful those abominable acts that we used to deem lawful. Then, when they subjugated us, wronged us, and treated us in an oppressive manner, standing between us and our religion, we came to your country, and we chose you over all other people. We desired to live alongside you, and we hoped that, with you, we would not be wronged, O king.' al-Najāshī said to Jaʿfar ﷺ, 'Do you have any of that which he came with from Allah?' Jaʿfar ﷺ said, 'Yes.' 'Then recite to me,' said al-Najāshī. Jaʿfar ﷺ recited for him the beginning of Sūrah Maryam. By Allah, al-Najāshī began to cry, until his beard became wet with tears. And when his priests heard what Jaʿfar ﷺ was reciting to them, they cried until their scrolls became wet. al-Najāshī then said, "By Allah, this and what Mūsa ﷺ came with come out of the same lantern. Then by Allah ﷻ, I will never surrender them to you, and henceforward they will not be plotted against and tortured."[4]

Describing what happened after the aforementioned discussion between al-Najāshī and Jaʿfar ﷺ, Umm Salamah ﷺ said, "When both ʿAmr ibn al-ʿĀṣ and ʿAbdullah ibn abī Rabīʿah left the presence of al-Najāshī, ʿAmr said, 'By Allah tomorrow I will present to him information about them with which I will pull up by the roots their very lives.' ʿAbdullah ibn Rabīʿah who was more sympathetic of the two towards us said, 'Don't do so, for they have certain rights of family relations, even if they have opposed us.' ʿAmr said, 'By Allah, I will inform him that they claim that ʿĪsā ibn Maryam is a slave.'

He went to the king on the following day and said, 'O king, verily, they have strong words to say about ʿĪsā ﷺ. Call them here and ask them what they say about him.' al-Najāshī sent for them in order to ask them about ʿĪsā ﷺ. Nothing similar to this befell us before. The group of Muslims gathered together and said to one another, 'What will you say about ʿĪsā ﷺ when he asks you about him?' They said, 'By Allah ﷻ, we will say about him that which Allah ﷻ says and that which our Prophet ﷺ came with, regardless of the outcome.' When they entered into his presence, he said to them, 'What do you say about ʿĪsā ibn Maryam?' Jaʿfar ﷺ said, 'We say about him that which our Prophet ﷺ came with - that he is the slave of Allah ﷻ, His messenger, a spirit created by Him, and His word, which he bestowed on Maryam, the virgin, the baṭūl.'

al-Najāshī struck his hand on the ground and took from it a stick. He then said, "ʿĪsā ibn Maryam did not go beyond what you said even the distance of the stick.' When he said this, his ministers spoke out in anger, to which he responded, 'What I said is true even if you speak out in anger, by Allah ﷻ. (Turning to the Muslims, he said) Go, for you are safe in my land.

4 Aḥmad, *Musnad*, 1740 and ibn Hishām, *Sīrah*, 1:336

Whoever curses you will be held responsible. And I would not love to have a reward of gold in return for me hurting a single man among you. (Speaking to his ministers he said) Return to these two (men) their gifts, since we have no need for them. For by Allah ﷻ, Allah ﷻ did not take from me bribe money when He returned to me my kingdom, so why should I take bribe money?' The two left, defeated and humiliated; and returned to them were the things they came with. We then resided alongside al-Najāshī in a very good abode, with a very good neighbor."[5]

This is such a beautiful, powerful, and profound event in the lives of the Companions that is full of several lessons, reminders, and benefits. Jaʿfar's ﷺ conversation with al-Najāshī and the support of the Companions that were with him is an amazing display of the strength of their īmān and reliance upon Allah ﷻ.

5 Aḥmad, *Musnad*, 1740

EXPLANATION OF SURAH MARYAM

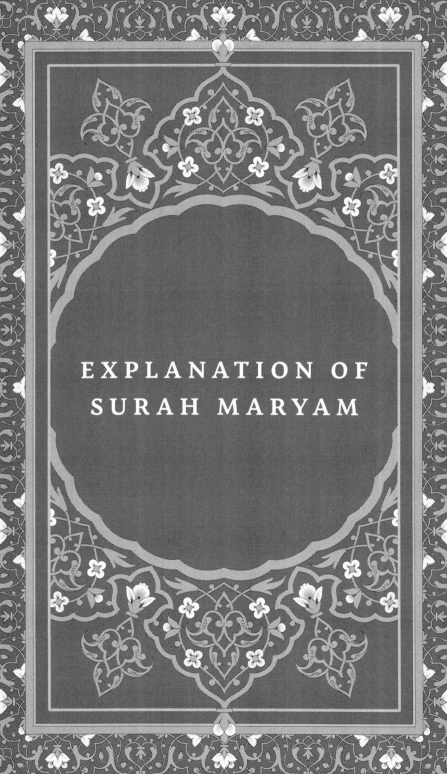

VERSE 1

كٓهيعٓصٓ ①

[1] Kāf, Hā, Yā, ʿAyn, Ṣād.

Allah ﷻ starts this beautiful Sūrah with a series of five letters that are recited separately. There are many different sayings or explanations regarding these five letters and what they mean. The most correct position is that these are from the separated letters (al-ḥurūf al-muqaṭṭaʿah). There are 29 different chapters in the Quran that start with separated letters. Allah ﷻ alone knows the meanings of these letters and He mentions them to highlight the miraculous and inimitable nature of the Quran. They are considered to be a secret from among the secrets of Allah ﷻ; meaning, no one knows what they truly mean except for the Creator Himself. They are from among the Mutashābihāt, those words or verses of the Quran whose meanings are hidden, unknown to us as human beings, or ambiguous. The definite meanings of these words and verses are unknown to us, highlighting our limited knowledge in comparison to the infinite and limitless knowledge of Allah ﷻ.

However, we do find that some great Companions of the Prophet ﷺ as well as their students sometimes gave meanings to these separated letters. For example, it's said that they are acronyms and each letter represents one of the names of Allah ﷻ. "Kāf" is for al-Kāfī (the All-Sufficient) or al-Karīm (the Most Noble), "hā" is for al-Hādī (the Guide), "yā" is taken from al-Ḥakīm (The Infinitely Wise) or al-Raḥīm (the Very Merciful), "ʿayn" is from al-ʿAlīm (the All-Knowing) or al-ʿAẓīm (the Almighty), and "ṣād" is from al-Ṣādiq (the Truthful). ibn ʿAbbās ﵄ narrated that, "'Kāf' is for Kāf (All-Sufficient), 'hā' is for Hād (the Guide), 'yā' is from Ḥakīm (All-Wise), 'ʿayn' is from ʿAlīm (All-Knowing), and 'ṣād' is from Ṣādiq (Truthful)."[6] Others have said that it is one of the names of Allah ﷻ and that it's actually the Greatest Name of Allah (al-Ism al-Aʿẓam), or that it's a name of the Quran. However, these narrations can't be used as proof or to assign definitive meanings. They offer possibilities, but no one truly knows what they mean.

Naturally, the question that comes to our minds is why would Allah ﷻ start a sūrah with words that no one understands? The Scholars of the Quran have offered the following possible reasons:

1. To grab the attention of the listeners. One of the responsibilities of the Prophet ﷺ was to recite revelation, the Quran, to his community. When he would start his recitation with a series of separated letters it would capture the attention and intrigue of his audience.
2. To remind us that no matter how much we know there's always something that we don't know. The unknown nature of the separated letters helps keep us grounded and creates a sense of intellectual humility. No matter how much we advance as human beings in terms of knowledge, now matter how much we explore, research, discover, and uncover, our knowledge is very limited. Human knowledge is nothing compared to the infinite and limitless knowledge of Allah ﷻ.
3. These letters are the letters of the Arabic Language, and the Quran was revealed at a time that was the peak of eloquence of the language

6 Qurṭubī, *al-Jāmiʿ lī Aḥkām al-Quran*, 13:404

and it was considered their identity. The Arabs took a lot of pride in their expertise in the Arabic Language, particularly composing prose and poetry that was extremely eloquent and beautiful. The Quran was revealed challenging them spiritually and intellectually. The Arabs never heard these letters being used in such a majestic and unique way.

4. To bring attention to the miraculous and inimitable nature of the Quran. Human beings can never match the power, eloquence, beauty, and style of the Quran.

Allah ﷻ then starts the story of Zakariyyā ﷺ, who is one of the Prophets sent to the Children of Israel. He is among the final group of Prophets that was sent to the Children of Israel preceding his son Yaḥyā ﷺ, and his relative through marriage, ʿIsā ﷺ. He is the husband of Maryam's ﷺ paternal aunt and one of the caretakers or custodians of Bayt al-Maqdis[7]. He also served as Maryam's ﷺ caretaker and guardian. It is reported that Maryam's ﷺ father, ʿImrān, passed away before she was born, and her mother, Ḥannah, had dedicated her child to the service of God and religion in Bayt al-Maqdis. The stories of Zakariyyā, Yaḥyā, Maryam, and ʿIsā ﷺ are interconnected.

VERSE 2

ذِكْرُ رَحْمَتِ رَبِّكَ عَبْدَهُۥ زَكَرِيَّآ

[This is] a reminder of the mercy of your Lord to His servant Zakariyyā.

7 Bayt al-Maqdis, or the Sacred House, is a title for the Temple in Jerusalem, which is where the original Temple of Sulaimān ﷺ was located. In the modern era, it is a name for the entire al-Aqṣā compound that includes both the Dome of the Rock and Masjid al-Aqṣā.

Allah ﷻ introduces the story of Zakariyyā ﷺ in a very brief and succinct way, highlighting its main theme and topic, which is Allah's infinite and limitless mercy. This is a unique style that Allah ﷻ uses when mentioning stories in the Quran. He starts by giving a brief overview or summary followed by a more detailed account. This is done to build interest and intrigue in the hearts and minds of the audience.

The word "dhikr" literally means remembrance, mention, or reminder. In this verse, grammatically speaking, it is the predicate of the sentence. The subject hasn't been mentioned but is understood from the context. The meaning is that what is being recited is a reminder of your Lord's mercy to His servant Zakariyyā ﷺ or that this is a reminder of your Lord's mercy to His servant Zakariyyā ﷺ, as is shown in the translation. Omitting the subject and mentioning the predicate is a literary technique used to draw attention and give importance to the predicate itself. It's being used here to draw our attention to the mercy of Allah ﷻ and how that mercy was shown to Zakariyyā ﷺ.

Zakariyyā ﷺ was a Prophet sent to the Children of Israel. He has been mentioned in eight different places throughout the Quran. It is mentioned in a few narrations that he was a carpenter and earned a livelihood through carpentry. He was Maryam's ﷺ uncle, married to her maternal aunt, and he was the one chosen to look after her. Zakariyyā ﷺ was a recipient of Allah's infinite grace and mercy in a very unique and special situation. Zakariyyā ﷺ and his wife were blessed with a child at a very old age, when it seemed nearly impossible to do so. Allah ﷻ showered His mercy upon him by blessing him and his wife with a child in these seemingly impossible circumstances.

One of the reasons why Allah ﷻ is drawing attention to this fact is to remind the Prophet ﷺ that he will also receive the mercy of Allah ﷻ despite the current circumstance if he continues to ask Allah ﷻ. Allah ﷻ introduced the story and it's main lesson in this verse and now He mentions the story in detail.

VERSE 3

إِذْ نَادَىٰ رَبَّهُۥ نِدَآءً خَفِيًّا

When he called to his Lord a private supplication.

In this verse, Allah ﷻ is addressing the Prophet ﷺ directly. Remember when Zakariyyā ﷺ supplicated to his Lord privately. Whenever "idh" is mentioned in the Quran, the verb "remember" is understood to come before it. This verse and the story serves as a form of consolation and reassurance for the Prophet ﷺ. It is as if Allah ﷻ is comforting him through Zakariyyā's ﷺ story and reminding him to remain patient and place his trust in Him alone.

Allah ﷻ is telling us that Zakariyyā ﷺ made duʿā, supplication, calling out to Allah ﷻ in seclusion in a lowered voice. From this verse we learn some of the etiquettes of supplication. It should be made silently in private without ostentation. Duʿā is a private affair between Allah ﷻ and us. It's a private conversation between us and our Lord and Creator and an opportunity for us to open our hearts to Allah ﷻ and tell Him about all of our worries and concerns. We share both our hopes and fears with the Most Merciful. Oftentimes by doing so we find comfort, relief, reassurance and solace. Allah ﷻ then tells us what he made duʿā for; what he actually said.

VERSE 4

قَالَ رَبِّ إِنِّي وَهَنَ ٱلْعَظْمُ مِنِّي وَٱشْتَعَلَ ٱلرَّأْسُ شَيْبًا وَلَمْ أَكُن
بِدُعَآئِكَ رَبِّ شَقِيًّا

He said, "My Lord, indeed my bones have grown weak, and my head has flared up with white hair, and I have never been disappointed in my supplication to You, my Lord.

Zakariyyā ﷺ starts his supplication by humbling himself before Allah ﷻ by describing his physical weakness due to old age. He's mentioning some of the reasons why he's turning to Allah ﷻ for help; the causes that have compelled him to call out in private. As we learn from a few narrations, Allah ﷻ answers the call of the compelled.

He said, "My Lord, indeed my bones have grown weak." The verb "wahana" means to become weak and feeble, specifically in terms of bodily strength. As people grow old, they start to lose their physical abilities and strength. People at the age of sixty are physically very different than they were at the age of twenty. Their joints and bodies start aching and they slow down significantly. They are no longer able to move as they used to when they were younger. He's describing how he has become weak and frail in his old age.

He ﷺ adds, "And my head has flared up with white hair." The verb ishtaʿala literally means to catch fire, start burning, ignite, flare up, and blaze. It is generally used with fire to convey the meaning that the fire has become intense. This is a very eloquent and descriptive way of saying all of my hair has turned white. It's as if my head has caught fire with white hair and it has spread quickly without leaving anything.

Zakariyyā ﵇ is supplicating to Allah ﷻ in a very beautiful and intimate way, teaching us some of the etiquettes and manners of asking Allah ﷻ. He's speaking to Allah ﷻ in such a way that highlights the nature of their relationship. He recognizes that Allah ﷻ is close to him and that He responds to the call of His servants. Our supplications are intimate conversations with Allah ﷻ and we can be vulnerable with Him, sharing our feelings and emotions. This is a way of humbling ourselves before Allah ﷻ and realizing that we are weak and that Allah ﷻ is the Almighty.

He ﵇ then praises Allah's ﷻ generosity by acknowledging His grace and mercy through the previous favors and blessings He has bestowed upon him. "And I have never been disappointed in my supplication to You, my Lord." This means that in the past Allah ﷻ had always answered his prayers. Every time I have called upon you in the past, You have always responded and fulfilled my requests. Zakariyyā ﵇ is expressing hope and certainty in Allah ﷻ. He is expressing the hope and desire that his supplication will be accepted, just as all his previous supplications had been accepted. Zakariyyā ﵇ then mentions two of the reasons why he's making duʿā and the actual request itself.

VERSE 5

وَإِنِّى خِفْتُ ٱلْمَوَٰلِىَ مِن وَرَآءِى وَكَانَتِ ٱمْرَأَتِى عَاقِرًا فَهَبْ لِى مِن
لَّدُنكَ وَلِيًّا

Truly I fear [for] my successors (relatives) after me, and my wife has been barren, so grant me from Yourself an heir...

"Truly I fear [for] my successors (relatives) after me." Zakariyyā ﷇ has reached the end of his life, he has grown extremely old and weak, and he fears and has concern for his successors, relatives, and family that will come after him. He had genuine and sincere concern for their commitment to their faith and way of life. He wasn't sure what would happen to them after he left this world. He feared that they may not be able to remain steadfast upon their religion and hold on firmly to his teachings. He feared that they may drift away from their faith and way of life and lose their religion.

"And my wife has been barren." He's telling Allah ﷻ that his wife has been unable to bear him children. He didn't have a son whom he could train, educate, and nurture for the important task of carrying on the message of Allah ﷻ. Zakariyya's ﷇ wife was Maryam's ﷇ maternal aunt, Ḥannah's sister, who is Maryam's ﷇ mother. Her name is mentioned as Īshāʿ the daughter of Fāqūdhā. After humbling himself before Allah ﷻ and mentioning why he feels compelled to ask, he now makes the request.

"So grant me from Yourself an heir." Meaning, O my Lord! Gift me with the special gift of a child. He's not asking for a child to show off or to carry on his lineage and legacy, but for the preservation of faith. He ﷇ describes the child saying,

VERSE 6

يَرِثُنِي وَيَرِثُ مِنْ ءَالِ يَعْقُوبَ ۖ وَٱجْعَلْهُ رَبِّ رَضِيًّا

who will inherit from me and inherit from the family of Yaʿqūb. And make him, my Lord, pleasing [to You]."

He ؑ describes the child as someone who will inherit from him and from the family of Yaʿqūb ؑ. What exactly he wants him to inherit isn't mentioned explicitly. According to most scholars, it's not prophethood because prophethood is something that can't be inherited; it is not passed on from generation to generation. It's something that Allah ﷻ chooses to give to select people. Most scholars also say that it's not wealth because the Prophet's didn't leave behind material wealth as inheritance. It's referring to knowledge, wisdom, character, morals, and religion. He's asking Allah ﷻ to grant him a child that will have deep knowledge and understanding of religion, excellent character, and impeccable morals. Allah ﷻ mentions his duʿā in Sūrah Āl ʿImrān saying, "Then and there Zakariyyā prayed to his Lord, saying, 'My Lord! Grant me—by your grace—righteous offspring. You are certainly the Hearer of [all] prayers.'"[8]

"And make him, my Lord, pleasing [to You]." He's asking Allah ﷻ to make this child pleasing to Him in terms of his speech, actions, and manners and to make him pleased with Allah ﷻ in terms of what He decrees for him. Meaning someone who is accepted by Allah ﷻ, is pleased with Allah ﷻ, and is also accepted by people. This is a very important point; his desire to have a son wasn't based on human want or desire. He wanted a child because he was genuinely concerned for his people, their faith, and salvation. He asked for a child to carry on his legacy of Prophethood and to propagate the message of dīn.

Zakariyyā ؑ was motivated to make this supplication while he was caring for Maryam ؑ. Allah ﷻ tells us in Sūrah Āl ʿImrān, "So her Lord accepted her graciously and blessed her with a pleasant upbringing—entrusting her to the care of Zakariyyā. Whenever Zakariyyā visited her in the sanctuary, he found her supplied with provisions. He exclaimed, 'O Maryam! Where did this come from?' She replied, 'It is from Allah. Surely Allah provides for whoever He wills without limit.'"[9] Witnessing these unique blessings and provisions that Allah ﷻ bestowed upon Maryam ؑ and the strength of her belief and reliance upon Allah ﷻ, served as a catalyst, a motivating factor, for Zakariyyā ؑ to supplicate to Allah ﷻ for a child that would carry on his

---

8 هُنَالِكَ دَعَا زَكَرِيَّا رَبَّهُ ۖ قَالَ رَبِّ هَبْ لِي مِن لَّدُنكَ ذُرِّيَّةً طَيِّبَةً ۖ إِنَّكَ سَمِيعُ الدُّعَاءِ - 3:38

9 فَتَقَبَّلَهَا رَبُّهَا بِقَبُولٍ حَسَنٍ وَأَنبَتَهَا نَبَاتًا حَسَنًا وَكَفَّلَهَا زَكَرِيَّا ۖ كُلَّمَا دَخَلَ عَلَيْهَا زَكَرِيَّا الْمِحْرَابَ وَجَدَ عِندَهَا رِزْقًا ۖ قَالَ يَا مَرْيَمُ أَنَّىٰ لَكِ هَٰذَا ۖ قَالَتْ هُوَ مِنْ عِندِ اللَّهِ ۖ إِنَّ اللَّهَ يَرْزُقُ مَن يَشَاءُ بِغَيْرِ حِسَابٍ - 3:37

legacy. Allah ﷻ says, “Then and there Zakariyyā prayed to his Lord, saying, ‘My Lord! Grant me—by your grace—righteous offspring. You are certainly the Hearer of ⌜all⌝ prayers.’”[10] Allah ﷻ then tells us how He responded.

VERSE 7

يَٰزَكَرِيَّآ إِنَّا نُبَشِّرُكَ بِغُلَٰمٍ ٱسْمُهُۥ يَحْيَىٰ لَمْ نَجْعَل لَّهُۥ مِن قَبْلُ سَمِيًّا

[He was told], "O Zakariyyā, truly We give you good news of a boy whose name will be John. We have not given this as a name to anyone before him."

Allah ﷻ responded to Zakariyyā’s عليه السلام supplication and revealed to him that he will be receiving the good news of a son named Yaḥyā (John). Not only did Allah ﷻ bless him with a son but He also chose his name, which is a very unique and distinct honor. The name Yaḥyā was unique; no one had ever been named that before. It also means that he was given some special gifts that no other Prophet was given. For example, he was granted prophethood while he was still a child, he was chaste, and was born from parents who were barren until then. This verse shows the status of Zakariyyā عليه السلام and the mercy that Allah ﷻ bestowed upon him. In Sūrah Āl ‘Imrān Allah ﷻ says, “So the angels called out to him while he stood praying in the sanctuary, ‘Allah gives you good news of [the birth of] Yaḥyā who will confirm the Word of Allah and will be a great leader, chaste, and a prophet

10 هُنَالِكَ دَعَا زَكَرِيَّا رَبَّهُۥ ۖ قَالَ رَبِّ هَبْ لِى مِن لَّدُنكَ ذُرِّيَّةً طَيِّبَةً ۖ إِنَّكَ سَمِيعُ ٱلدُّعَآءِ - 3:38

among the righteous.'"[11]

Zakariyyā ﷺ was astonished and amazed by this news. It was almost as if he was caught off guard. He believed it for sure, he had absolutely no doubts about it whatsoever, but wanted to know more. The feeling can be compared to a student who hasn't prepared for an exam. They take the exam thinking that they failed it miserably. When they receive the results, they find out that they got an A. This student is going to be astonished, amazed, surprised, and shocked. He's going to want to know how this happened and how it's possible. Those were the emotions and thoughts running through Zakariyyā's ﷺ heart and mind.

VERSE 8

قَالَ رَبِّ أَنَّىٰ يَكُونُ لِي غُلَامٌ وَكَانَتِ ٱمْرَأَتِي عَاقِرًا وَقَدْ بَلَغْتُ مِنَ ٱلْكِبَرِ عِتِيًّا

He said, "My Lord, how will I have a boy when my wife is barren and I have reached extreme old age?"

Zakariyyā ﷺ is expressing amazement and wonder at this great news. How is it possible for me to have a child when my wife is unable to do so and I'm so old? He's not doubting the news, but he's excited and wants to know how. Allah ﷻ narrates this portion of the story in Sūrah Āl ʿImrān saying, "He exclaimed, 'My Lord! How can I have a son when I am very old and my wife is barren?' He replied, 'So will it be. Allah does what He

11 فَنَادَتْهُ الْمَلَائِكَةُ وَهُوَ قَائِمٌ يُصَلِّي فِي الْمِحْرَابِ أَنَّ اللَّهَ يُبَشِّرُكَ بِيَحْيَىٰ مُصَدِّقًا - 3:39 بِكَلِمَةٍ مِّنَ اللَّهِ وَسَيِّدًا وَحَصُورًا وَنَبِيًّا مِّنَ الصَّالِحِينَ

wills.'"[12] Allah ﷻ responds to him with a very simple and direct reminder of His ultimate might, power, and magnificence.

VERSE 9

قَالَ كَذَٰلِكَ قَالَ رَبُّكَ هُوَ عَلَيَّ هَيِّنٌ وَقَدْ خَلَقْتُكَ مِن قَبْلُ وَلَمْ تَكُ شَيْـًٔا

He said, "So it is. Your Lord says, 'It is easy for Me, just as I created you before, when you were nothing!'"

"He said, 'So it is.'" Meaning, you will have a child even though you're so old and your wife until now has been unable to bear children. Allah ﷻ then says "it is easy for Me," reminding Zakariyyā ؑ of His ultimate and infinite might and power. He is telling him that for Me to grant you a son despite the impossible circumstances is something simple and easy. In order for us to completely understand this truth and reality - the ultimate and infinite might and power of Allah ﷻ - He ﷻ reminds Zakariyyā ؑ, "I created you before, when you were nothing." I created you and brought you into this world from nothing; specifically, the father of humanity Adam ؑ, and from him I created many men and women. This verse helps us develop a better understanding of Allah ﷻ being al-Khāliq, the Creator. He ﷻ alone is the Creator of the universe and every single thing it contains.

Syed Quṭb ؒ comments on this verse saying, "With regard to creation,

12 3:40 - قَالَ رَبِّ أَنَّىٰ يَكُونُ لِي غُلَامٌ وَقَدْ بَلَغَنِيَ الْكِبَرُ وَامْرَأَتِي عَاقِرٌ ۖ قَالَ كَذَٰلِكَ اللَّهُ يَفْعَلُ مَا يَشَاءُ

there is nothing to be classified as easy or difficult in as far as God is concerned. In all cases of creation, whether it is something large or small, trivial or gigantic, the method is the same: it is only a matter of God willing that thing to be and it comes into existence. It is God who makes a barren woman childless, and an old man unable to procreate. He is certainly able to reverse this situation, removing the cause of a woman's barrenness and renewing a man's ability to cause his wife to conceive. By human standards, this is easier than initiating life in the first place. But with God, everything is easy, whether it involves origination or rebirth."[13]

After hearing this good news, Zakariyyā ﷺ was in a state of wonder, amazement, excitement, and shock. In this emotional state, he asked Allah ﷻ when this would happen.

VERSE 10

قَالَ رَبِّ ٱجْعَل لِّىٓ ءَايَةً ۚ قَالَ ءَايَتُكَ أَلَّا تُكَلِّمَ ٱلنَّاسَ ثَلَٰثَ لَيَالٍ سَوِيًّا

He said, "My Lord, grant me a sign." He said, "Your sign is that you will not speak to the people for three nights, despite being healthy."

Zakariyyā ﷺ asked Allah ﷻ to give him some sort of sign or indication as to when this will happen. Tell me when my wife will become pregnant? It's important to recognize that he's not asking because he's impatient, but rather because of his happiness, joy, and excitement. Allah ﷻ

---

13 Quṭb, *fī Ẓilāl al-Quran*, 4:2303

responded by telling him that when his wife becomes expectant, he won't be able to speak for three days and three nights. His inability to speak will not be the result of an illness or any other apparent cause; he will be perfectly fine and healthy. Allah ﷻ will temporarily remove his ability to speak as a sign of this great news. The reason why this is considered a sign is because there will be nothing wrong with Zakariyyā ﵇, he will be perfectly healthy, but Allah ﷻ will not allow him to speak and converse with people for three days and nights. This is similar to what Allah ﷻ says in Sūrah Āl ʿImrān, "He said, 'My Lord, give me a sign.' 'Your sign,' [the Angel] said, 'is that you will not communicate with anyone for three days, except by gestures. Remember your Lord often; celebrate His glory in the evening and at dawn.'"[14]

VERSE 11

فَخَرَجَ عَلَىٰ قَوْمِهِۦ مِنَ ٱلْمِحْرَابِ فَأَوْحَىٰٓ إِلَيْهِمْ أَن سَبِّحُوا۟ بُكْرَةً
وَعَشِيًّا

So he came out to his people from the prayer chamber (sanctuary) and signaled to them that they should glorify [Allah] morning and evening.

In this verse Allah ﷻ is telling us what happened when this sign that was given to Zakariyyā ﵇ that his wife was expecting appeared. Zakariyyā ﵇, in addition to being a carpenter by trade, was one of the caretakers of Bayt al-Maqdis. Within the structure he had a particular miḥrāb, which

14 3:41 - قَالَ رَبِّ ٱجْعَل لِّىٓ ءَايَةً ۖ قَالَ ءَايَتُكَ أَلَّا تُكَلِّمَ ٱلنَّاسَ ثَلَٰثَةَ أَيَّامٍ إِلَّا رَمْزًا ۗ وَٱذْكُر رَّبَّكَ كَثِيرًا وَسَبِّحْ بِٱلْعَشِىِّ وَٱلْإِبْكَٰرِ

can be understood as a personal or private prayer space. It is in this miḥrāb that he supplicated to Allah ﷻ and received the good news of being blessed with a child who will be named Yaḥyā. It is mentioned in some narrations that as a caretaker and Prophet, he would open Bayt al-Maqdis for the morning and late afternoon prayers. One day he came out of his private prayer space to open Bayt al-Maqdis and lead his people in prayer when he found that he was unable to speak. This is the sign he was promised and what he had been waiting for. Unable to speak, he used gestures and signs telling them to continue glorifying Allah ﷻ in the morning and late afternoon.

LESSONS AND BENEFITS FROM THE STORY OF ZAKARIYYĀ عليه السلام

There are several lessons and benefits that can be derived from this portion of Zakariyyā's عليه السلام story:

1.

Consolation and Reassurance - Allah ﷻ mentions the stories of several past Prophets, Messengers, and communities throughout the Quran. The purpose of these stories is not to simply provide historical information. Allah ﷻ mentions these stories for us to read, study, analyze, and derive practical morals, lessons, and guidance. As Allah ﷻ says in Sūrah Yūsuf, "In their stories there is truly a lesson for people of reason. This message cannot be a fabrication, rather [it is] a confirmation of previous revelation, a detailed explanation of all things, a guide, and a mercy for people of faith."[15] The stories are oftentimes also mentioned to console, comfort, and reassure the Prophet ﷺ and his followers. Allah ﷻ says in Sūrah Hūd, "And We relate to you [O Prophet] the stories of the Messengers to reassure your heart. And there has come to you in this [sūrah] the truth, a warning [to the disbelievers], and a reminder to the believers."[16] Here Allah ﷻ mentions Zakariyyā's عليه السلام story as

---

15 12:111 - لَقَدْ كَانَ فِي قَصَصِهِمْ عِبْرَةٌ لِّأُولِي الْأَلْبَابِ ۗ مَا كَانَ حَدِيثًا يُفْتَرَىٰ وَلَٰكِن تَصْدِيقَ الَّذِي بَيْنَ يَدَيْهِ وَتَفْصِيلَ كُلِّ شَيْءٍ وَهُدًى وَرَحْمَةً لِّقَوْمٍ يُؤْمِنُونَ

16 11:120 - وَكُلًّا نَّقُصُّ عَلَيْكَ مِنْ أَنبَاءِ الرُّسُلِ مَا نُثَبِّتُ بِهِ فُؤَادَكَ ۚ وَجَاءَكَ فِي هَٰذِهِ الْحَقُّ وَمَوْعِظَةٌ وَذِكْرَىٰ لِلْمُؤْمِنِينَ

a source of consolation and reassurance for the Prophet ﷺ, his companions, and those that come after them.

2.

The Power of Duʿā - This story highlights the amazing power of a sincere duʿā. Duʿā, supplication, calling upon Allah ﷻ, is one of the absolute most powerful tools that a believer has. The Prophet ﷺ said, "Dua is the weapon of the believer."[17] It is a direct line of communication between a believer and their Lord and Creator. It is considered to be the essence or epitome of worship. The Prophet ﷺ teaches us, "If you ask, ask Allah."[18] We are supposed to turn towards Allah ﷻ and to ask Him alone for all of our needs. People should be completely dependent upon Allah ﷻ, not His creation, because it is Allah ﷻ and Allah ﷻ alone who is able to take care of all needs.

3.

Overcoming Impossible Circumstances - This is a very instructive story showing us that it is possible to overcome seemingly impossible circumstances with the help, assistance, aid, and support of Allah ﷻ.

4.

Reliance upon Allah ﷻ - Zakariyyā ﷺ is a prime example of what tawakkul looks like in real life. The reality of tawakkul is recognizing with absolute firm conviction and certainty that nothing and no one in this world can cause harm or benefit, give or take, without the decree, will, and permission of Allah ﷻ. It includes relegating the consequences of one's affairs to Allah ﷻ, relying upon His help, and trusting and accepting His decisions.

5.

The Ultimate Might and Power of Allah ﷻ - Yaḥyā's ﷺ birth to extremely old parents, particularly a mother who had formerly been barren, highlights the ultimate might and power of Allah ﷻ. His ﷻ power to create transcends and goes far beyond all ordinary physical limitations. Human limitations and boundaries are immaterial to the manifestation of God's might and power.

---

17 al-Mundhirī, *al-Targhīb wa al-Tarhīb*, 2:390

18 Tirmidhī, *k. ṣifah al-qiyāmah wa al-raqā'iq wa al-warʿ ʿan rasūlillah*, 2706

6.

Etiquettes of Duʿā - Zakariyyā ﷺ demonstrates some essential etiquettes of supplicating to Allah ﷻ. When we supplicate to Allah ﷻ we should humble ourselves and recognize that we are calling upon the Almighty, the All-Powerful Who, when He wants to create something, says be and it is. We should also start our supplications by praising Allah ﷻ and expressing gratitude for His blessings and favors that He has bestowed upon us.

7.

al-Raḥmah - As mentioned earlier, this is the central theme of the entire Sūrah. Here we see Allah's ﷻ raḥmah expressed as granting Zakariyyā ﷺ and his wife a righteous child despite their extremely old age. Not only was this a mercy upon them, but it was also a mercy upon the community because their child, Yaḥyā ﷺ, was also a Prophet.

8.

Sincere Concern for the Spiritual Well-Being of Future Generations - Through this story we learn that we shouldn't only be concerned with ourselves or our families. Rather, we should be concerned for the entire community, particularly its spiritual well-being.

After mentioning the story of Zakariyyā ⛤, Allah ⛤ immediately changes the subject to Yaḥyā ⛤ and some of his unique qualities and characteristics.

VERSE 12

يَٰيَحْيَىٰ خُذِ ٱلْكِتَٰبَ بِقُوَّةٍ ۖ وَءَاتَيْنَٰهُ ٱلْحُكْمَ صَبِيًّا

"O Yaḥyā, hold on to the Scripture firmly." And We gave him wisdom as a child.

We have now fast-forwarded slightly in the story. Yaḥyā ⛤ is born and Allah ⛤ is now addressing him. Allah ⛤ says "O Yaḥyā, hold on to the Scripture firmly." The scripture being referred to here is the Torah. What is meant by holding on to it firmly is to read, study, understand, and teach it. Try your best to follow its guidance and remain steadfast upon its teachings while observing its commands and staying away from its prohibitions. Allah ﷻ also tells us that he gave Yaḥyā ﷺ wisdom and understanding while he was still a child. The word used in the verse is "al-ḥukm" and it has been explained in a few different ways. Some mention that it's referring to a deep understanding of faith and religion and an inclination towards righteousness. Others are of the opinion that it is referring to Prophethood. It's mentioned in a narration that once a boy came to Yaḥyā ﷺ and said let's go play. He replied, "We haven't been created to play," and that is why Allah ﷻ said, "And We gave him wisdom as a child."[19] Allah ﷻ then mentions some of the unique favors He blessed him with.

VERSE 13

وَحَنَانًا مِّن لَّدُنَّا وَزَكَوٰةً ۖ وَكَانَ تَقِيًّا

And tenderness from Us and purity, and he was fearing of Allah.

The word "ḥanān" literally means affection. It includes mercy, love, sympathy, tenderness, and kindness. It conveys the meaning of a gentle mercy and compassion. Yaḥyā ﷺ was showered with mercy and compassion from Allah ﷻ and he dealt with people and interacted with them with mercy and compassion. This one word description highlights that he had excellent manners and dealt with people in the best way possible. His father Zakariyyā ﷺ made sure he had the best tarbiyyah, the best upbringing, knowing how to show compassion to the young and respect to the elders. The concept of "ḥanān" is referring to his akhlāq (manners), which

19 Qurṭubī, *al-Jamiʿ lī Aḥkām al-Quran*, 13:423

is an essential part of a believers identity. It is also one of the most important qualities for a Prophet to possess because they are dealing with people's hearts and souls, gently guiding them towards what's best for them in this world and the next.

"Zakāh" literally means purity. Here it's referring to spiritual purity; the fact that he was pure from any sins, diseases of the heart, and moral defects. "Zakā" is the origin of the word tazkiyah, which refers to spirituality and purification of the heart, which is an integral part of one's relationship with Allah ﷻ and others. Yaḥyā ﵇ was free from spiritual ailments and diseases such as hypocrisy, jealousy, greed, hatred, pride, arrogance, doubt, cowardice, miserliness, ostentation, and love of this world.

Allah ﷻ ends the verse saying, "And he was fearing of Allah." The word "taqiyy" refers to someone who is extremely God-conscious and God-fearing. Yaḥyā ﵇ is being described as a person of taqwā. He has an extremely strong relationship with Allah ﷻ and tried his best to obey all His commandments and stay away from all His prohibitions.

In this verse, Allah ﷻ has described Yaḥyā ﵇ with three unique qualities and characteristics that helped him serve and fulfill his role as a Prophet:

1. kindness and compassion
2. purity, and
3. God consciousness

Allah ﷻ then describes him with two more special qualities.

VERSE 14

وَبَرًّا بِوَالِدَيْهِ وَلَمْ يَكُن جَبَّارًا عَصِيًّا

And dutiful to his parents, and he was not domineering, rebellious.

"Barr" comes from the word "birr," which means righteousness. This is an exaggerated form of the word. In the Quran, it's used in connection to how one deals with their parents. It gives the meaning of being obedient, loving, respectful, and dutiful to one's parents. Birr al-Wālidayn (righteousness with one's parents) includes serving one's parents, listening to them, taking care of them, dealing with them with humility, gentleness, compassion, and care, showing them honor, and fulfilling their needs and necessities. It can be understood as general good conduct towards one's parents. Allah ﷻ is praising Yaḥyā ﷺ as being someone who treats his parents in the best way possible.

"And he was not domineering, rebellious." Yaḥyā ﷺ was a man of humility; he was not arrogant, prideful, or disobedient. He was the opposite; gentle, humble, and obedient. Saʿīd ibn al-Musayyab ﷺ narrates that the Messenger of Allah ﷺ said, "Everyone who meets Allah on the Day of Judgment will have some sin except for Yaḥyā ibn Zakariyyā."[20]

VERSE 15

وَسَلَٰمٌ عَلَيْهِ يَوْمَ وُلِدَ وَيَوْمَ يَمُوتُ وَيَوْمَ يُبْعَثُ حَيًّا

And safety and protection are upon him the day he was born and the day he dies and the day he is raised alive.

20 Ibn Kathīr, *Tafsīr al-Quran al-ʿAẓīm*,

After describing Yaḥyā 🕊 with all of these praiseworthy qualities, Allah 🕊 mentions some of their benefits and rewards. He will receive a triple blessing of "salām," which is best translated as safety, security, and protection. He was granted "salām" the day he was born, the day he passed away, and will be granted it the day he is brought back to life. This is almost identical to 'Isā's 🕊 statement about himself mentioned a little later in verse 33. The day he was born he was protected and granted security from the evil promptings of Satan. The day he passes away he will be protected from punishment in the grave and the day he's resurrected he will be protected from the trials and horrors of the Day of Judgment. Sufyān ibn 'Uyaynah 🕊 said, "A person experiences the most fright and loneliness in three instances: the day they are born because they are brought into a new environment, the day they die because they will see creatures they had never seen before, and the day they are resurrected when they find themselves gathered will all of humanity. Allah 🕊 favored Yaḥyā 🕊 by granting him salām during all three instances."[21]

LESSONS AND BENEFITS FROM THE STORY OF YAḤYĀ 🕊

1.

Holding on Firmly to Scripture - The story of Yaḥyā 🕊 indicates towards the importance and significance of holding on tightly to Scripture, which in our case is the Quran, the last and final revelation sent for the guidance of humanity until the end of times. It is essential for every single one of us to nurture, develop, and build a relationship with the Quran by reciting it regularly, reflecting and pondering over its meanings, and implementing its teachings and guidance into our daily lives.

2.

Wisdom - Wisdom has been described in several different ways. The most common definition given is putting things in their proper place. Usually, wisdom is acquired with time and experience. That is why elders are

---

21   Zuḥailī, *al-Tafsīr al-Munīr*, 8:399

generally considered to be more wise than those who are young. There's no better teacher than experience. Although this may be a cliche, its general meaning is true. Abū Saʿīd al-Khudrī ﵁ said, "There is no wise person without experience." [22]

3.

Good Character - Allah ﷻ describes Yaḥyā ﵇ as being blessed with "ḥanān," which can be understood as an aspect of good character. The importance of good character as part of one's Muslim identity cannot be overemphasized. Good character includes how a person speaks and behaves; their conduct and behavior especially with others. We should try our best to adorn our speech and behavior with noble qualities and characteristics such as gentleness, humility, compassion, sympathy, care, concern, patience, forbearance, and mercy. The Prophet ﷺ described perfecting good manners as the reason why he was sent as a Prophet. "I have only been sent to perfect good character."[23] Through this statement the Prophet ﷺ explained that one of the primary objectives of his mission was to perfect good character.

4.

Spiritual Purification - Tazkiyah, which is understood as spirituality and purification of the heart, is an integral part of our practice of Islam. Allah ﷻ describes it as one of the primary responsibilities of the Prophet ﷺ. Allah ﷻ says, "God has been truly gracious to the believers in sending them a Messenger from among their own, to recite His revelations to them, to make them grow in purity, and to teach them the Scripture and wisdom- before that they were clearly astray."[24] We have both praiseworthy and blameworthy characteristics and qualities. Our responsibility is to cleanse our hearts from blameworthy qualities and adorn them with praiseworthy qualities. We should work on purifying our hearts from spiritual ailments and diseases such as hypocrisy, jealousy, greed, hatred, pride, arrogance, doubt, cowardice, miserliness, ostentation, and love of this world. We should try our best to replace them with truthfulness, love, selflessness, humility, certainty,

22 Tirmidhī, *k. al-birr wa al-ṣilah ʿan rasūlillah, b. mā jā'a fī al-tajārib*, 2033

23 Haythamī, *Majmaʿ al-Zawā'id*, 9:18

24 لَقَدْ مَنَّ اللَّهُ عَلَى الْمُؤْمِنِينَ إِذْ بَعَثَ فِيهِمْ رَسُولًا مِّنْ أَنفُسِهِمْ يَتْلُو عَلَيْهِمْ آيَاتِهِ وَيُزَكِّيهِمْ وَيُعَلِّمُهُمُ الْكِتَابَ وَالْحِكْمَةَ وَإِن كَانُوا مِن قَبْلُ لَفِي ضَلَالٍ مُّبِينٍ - 3:164

bravery, generosity, sincerity, and simplicity.

5.

Taqwā - God-Consciousness, being aware of Allah ﷻ, is one of the greatest and most important qualities that a person is supposed to develop and nurture within themselves. It is described as a comprehensive trait that gathers all forms of good and protects one from all types of harm. It is one of the most essential aspects of a person's relationship with Allah ﷻ and is considered to be the catalyst behind everything a person does. In practical terms it is defined as obeying the commandments of Allah ﷻ and staying away from His prohibitions.

6.

Birr al-Wālidayn - Oftentimes, when we think about Islam and religion in general, we think about ritual acts of worship. We think about praying, fasting, reading Quran, and coming to the masjid. We also think about rules and regulations, do's and don'ts, ḥalāl and ḥarām. These are very important and fundamental to our practice of Islam, but they are only part of Islam. They are only one part of our religious identity and practice.

One of the most important and significant aspects of Islam is our moral character and social behavior; how we deal with others. And within the sphere of social behavior, specifically in terms of relationships, one of the most important relationships we have is with our parents. In several places throughout the Quran, Allah ﷻ commands us to be kind and respectful to our parents. Allah ﷻ says in Sūrah al-Isrā, "Your Lord has commanded that you should worship none but Him, and that you be kind to your parents."[25] This is an actual command from Allah ﷻ. Just like it is an obligation to pray five times a day, fast the month of Ramaḍān, and perform ḥajj if one has the ability to do so, it is an obligation to be kind and dutiful to our parents. The verse also highlights that after our relationship with Allah ﷻ, the most important relationship we have in life is that with our parents. That is one of the reasons why the Prophet ﷺ highlighted being kind and respectful to our parents as being one of the most virtuous and rewarding things that we can do. ibn Masʿūd رضي الله عنه narrates that he asked the Prophet ﷺ, "Which deed is most beloved to Allah?" He replied, "Praying on time." I said, "Then what?"

---

25 وَقَضَىٰ رَبُّكَ أَلَّا تَعْبُدُوا إِلَّا إِيَّاهُ وَبِالْوَالِدَيْنِ إِحْسَانًا - 17:23

He ﷺ said, "Being good to parents." I said, "Then what?" He said, "Jihād in the path of Allah."[26]

7.

Humility - The word for humility in Arabic is al-tawāḍuʿ. Linguistically it means to lower or humble oneself; self-abasement. Humility is the opposite of arrogance and vanity. It means not wanting to be in charge, well-known, popular, or famous. It includes turning away from recognition, dislike of being praised and honored, being noble and generous, and avoiding vanity and arrogance.

Humility is a trait or characteristic that results from cleansing our hearts from pride, arrogance, and vanity and by recognizing our true place in this universe. An essential aspect of humility is realizing that the world doesn't revolve around us; that we're not the most important person in the world or that our voice and opinion don't have to be heard.

This is a very difficult quality for us to develop and have because as human beings we are naturally self-centered; we like to think the best about ourselves. It takes a lot of effort, self-restraint, and struggle to develop humility. That's why Allah ﷻ has praised the people of humility in the Quran. He has given them good news and told them that their reward is Paradise saying, "We grant the Home in the Hereafter to those who do not seek superiority on earth or spread corruption: the happy ending is awarded to those who are mindful of God." [27]

The idea of humility itself suggests the idea of lowering ourselves in front of others. And although that may literally be true, in reality we're raising ourselves above others. Whenever we behave with humility, Allah ﷻ elevates us both in this world and the next. As the Prophet ﷺ told us, "Whoever behaves with humility for the sake of Allah, Allah will elevate him."[28] When we behave with humility people are drawn towards us; they open up their hearts to us and respect us. Through our humility we're given honor, respect, and love in this world. In the Hereafter, Allah ﷻ will elevate our ranks and reward us with Paradise.

---

26 Bukhārī, *k. al-aḍab, b. qawl Allah wa waṣṣaina al-insān bī wālidaih*, 5970

27 تِلْكَ الدَّارُ الْآخِرَةُ نَجْعَلُهَا لِلَّذِينَ لَا يُرِيدُونَ عُلُوًّا فِي الْأَرْضِ وَلَا فَسَادًا ۚ وَالْعَاقِبَةُ لِلْمُتَّقِينَ - 28:83

28 Muslim, *k. al-birr wa al-ṣ-ilah wa al-ādāb, b. isṫiḥbāb al-ʿafw wa al-tawāḍuʿ*, 2588

8.

Parenting Ideals - Through this story, Allah ﷻ is highlighting what our concerns as parents are supposed to be for our children. Our primary concern should be for their faith and salvation; their success in the life of the Hereafter. Our burning concern should be to ensure that they'll be successful in the life to come.

Our parenting methods are supposed to develop good character, spirituality, God-consciousness, and respect for elders; all of the qualities that were found in Yaḥyā ﷺ. For a long time now we've had a trend in the Muslim community where we've moved away from these parenting ideals.

These ideals are still considered to be good but they've become secondary. Our concern has become our children's educational and financial well being. From the time a child starts school, all the way through university, parents are focused on getting the best for their children. We want them to go to the best pre-schools, the best school districts in elementary, middle, and high schools. We want them to get straight A's. We pour a lot of our time, effort, energy, and money making sure they succeed in this world. We'll pay for extra help; we'll make sure they wake up for school early, arrive on time, and finish their homework on time.

When they're in college, we'll try everything we can to make sure they get the best experience. If our children want to become doctors or lawyers, we'll even take loans for hundreds of thousands of dollars. This is natural; all of us want the best for our children and we want them to succeed.

However, compare all of these efforts with the time, effort, energy, and money we spend on our children's religious education and upbringing. It's so disproportionate that they can't even be compared. Religious education is an afterthought. We'll drive our children to the SAT prep class but won't drive them to the masjid to learn Quran. We want someone to come to our homes to do that. We'll spend thousands of dollars on their LSAT or MCAT prep course but we feel hesitant spending $100 a month for them to learn Arabic. We'll make sure they're up and ready before school starts so they can be there before the bell rings but we won't wake them up for Fajr.

As parents, especially as parents living in the West, we really have to shift our priorities. At least the same amount of time we put into our children's academic studies should be put into their religious studies, if not more. We have to be fair.

I'm not saying that any of these things are bad. They're all great. Our kids should be doctors, engineers, lawyers, journalists, and scientists. They should excel in this world. Along with that, they should also excel in their religion. It should make us proud that our children have good character, that they're spiritual, have taqwā, and are respectful. If we can develop that then we've guaranteed their success.

After mentioning the story of Zakariyyā ﷺ and how he was given a son despite it seeming like it was impossible, Allah ﷻ now mentions the story of Maryam and ʿIsā ﷺ, which is even more amazing and remarkable. The first story was a story of extremely old parents giving birth to a child despite the odds, and this story is about the miraculous birth of a child without a father. The same sequence is used in Sūrah Āl ʿImrān. Allah ﷻ is building up our faith step-by-step. Allah ﷻ starts this story by telling the Prophet ﷺ to remember the story himself and to mention it to others.

VERSE 16

وَٱذْكُرْ فِى ٱلْكِتَـٰبِ مَرْيَمَ إِذِ ٱنتَبَذَتْ مِنْ أَهْلِهَا مَكَانًا شَرْقِيًّا

And mention, [O Muḥammad], in the Book [the story of] Maryam, when she withdrew from her family to a place toward the east.

Allah is addressing the Prophet directly and telling him to remember and remind others of the story of Maryam, particularly when she secluded herself from her family in a place facing the East. She withdrew from her family and secluded herself for worship in the Sacred Mosque in Jerusalem facing the East. Ibn ʿAbbās mentions that's why the Christians face east when they worship.[29]

This is how Allah introduces the story of Maryam, the daughter of ʿImrān and Ḥannah, the mother of ʿIsā. She was from a noble and pure lineage that traced its roots back to the Prophet Dāwūd. She was an extremely righteous and pious woman who was dedicated by her mother from birth to the worship and service of Allah. Ḥannah promised to dedicate her child to the service of Allah through study, devotion, and worship. Maryam has been mentioned multiple times throughout the Quran especially in terms of her purity and nobility. This entire Sūrah is named after her highlighting her rank and status.[30] It is mentioned that the name Maryam means "maidservant of Allah."

VERSE 17

فَٱتَّخَذَتْ مِن دُونِهِمْ حِجَابًا فَأَرْسَلْنَآ إِلَيْهَا رُوحَنَا فَتَمَثَّلَ لَهَا
بَشَرًا سَوِيًّا

29 Qurṭubī, *al-Jāmiʿ lī Aḥkām al-Quran*, 13:428

30 It seems like the majority of scholars are of the opinion that Maryam was a righteous and pious woman selected by Allah to demonstrate His infinite might and power through the miraculous birth of ʿIsā. A few scholars, including Imām al-Qurṭubī, are of the opinion that she was a female prophet. This brings about a very interesting discussion regarding gender and prophets. Allah knows best.

And she took, in seclusion from them, a veil. Then We sent to her Our Spirit, and it assumed for her the likeness of a well-proportioned man.

"And she took, in seclusion from them, a veil." Meaning, when she secluded herself for worship and devotion, she set up a barrier or a curtain so that she could worship in privacy, allowing her to concentrate and focus. This type of seclusion is more conducive to sincerity and removes all distractions. While she was in this secluded space, devoted to worship, Allah ﷻ "sent to her Our Spirit." The vast majority of commentators are of the opinion that the Spirit is referring to the Angel Jibrīl ﷺ. The word "Spirit" has been attributed to Allah ﷻ to highlight the status and rank of the Angel Jibrīl ﷺ. When Jibrīl ﷺ came to her he changed his outward appearance, assuming the shape of "a well-proportioned man."

While she was busy and engaged in worship and prayer, Allah ﷻ sent Jibrīl ﷺ to her in the form of a handsome young man. "A well-proportioned man" is understood to mean handsome, young, and healthy who would not cause her to be frightened or startled.

There are a few reasons why Jibrīl ﷺ was sent in the form of a human being:

1. To not frighten Maryam - If he were sent in his original form, Maryam ﷺ would have been scared and would not be able to converse with him. Some of the commentators mention that humans can't see angels in their true shape because they will be overwhelmed by their appearance. An exception to this is our beloved Prophet Muḥammad ﷺ who saw Jibrīl ﷺ in his original form.
2. To test her - She's a young woman and all of a sudden a handsome young man shows up while she's secluded in a private space. As soon as she saw him, Maryam ﷺ became apprehensive of his intentions. She demonstrated a very high level of taqwā, ḥayā, and courage. She was a young woman, he was a young unknown man, and she had no idea who he was or what he wanted. Allah ﷻ reveals her reaction in the next verse.

VERSE 18

قَالَتْ إِنِّيٓ أَعُوذُ بِٱلرَّحْمَـٰنِ مِنكَ إِن كُنتَ تَقِيًّا

She said, "Indeed, I seek refuge in the Most Merciful from you, [so leave me], if you have any fear of Him."

When she saw this man, a complete stranger, she immediately sought refuge with Allah ﷻ, the Most Merciful, from him and reminded him to fear Allah ﷻ. She uses words to first seek Divine protection and then other words to strike the fear of Allah ﷻ into someone's heart. She first said, "I seek refuge in the Most Merciful from you." The reason why she chose the attribute al-Raḥmān is because she wanted Allah ﷻ to have mercy upon her by protecting her from any evil intentions the person may have had. Some narrations mention that when Jibrīl ﵇ heard these words he stepped back a little out of respect for Allah's ﷻ name. [31]

al-Istiʿādhah, seeking Divine protection, is an extremely powerful, effective, and practical way of protecting ourselves from harm. Ibn al-Qayyim ﵀ explained the meaning of aʿūdhu in a very beautiful way. He wrote, "Know that the verb ʿādha and its derivatives carry the meaning of being careful and wary, guarding and fortifying, being rescued and victorious. Its essential meaning is to flee from that which you fear will harm you to that which will safeguard you from it. This is why the one you seek refuge with is named maʿādh and malja' (the source of refuge and recourse)... Therefore the meaning of aʿūdhu is: I take refuge, guard myself, and take precaution... The one taking refuge seeks protection with the one he is seeking refuge with and sticks firmly to him. His heart attaches itself to him and holds firm just as the child sticks close to its father when threatened by an enemy. The same

31 Qurṭubī, *al-Jāmiʿ lī Aḥkām al-Quran*, 13:429

applies to the one taking refuge for he flees from his enemy who desires his destruction to his Lord, throwing himself between His Hands, holding firmly to Him, sticking close to Him and resorting to Him."[32]

She then says words to strike the fear of Allah into his heart, "if you have any fear of Him." These are extremely powerful and concise words that can be used to make a person think about the consequences of what they're about to do. She was telling him that if he truly feared Allah, then he wouldn't do anything with ill intentions. This verse shows her faith, chastity, and righteousness.

Jibrīl then responded, calming her down and telling her that he was not who she thought he was.

VERSE 19

قَالَ إِنَّمَآ أَنَا۠ رَسُولُ رَبِّكِ لِأَهَبَ لَكِ غُلَـٰمًا زَكِيًّا

He said, "I am only the messenger of your Lord to give you the gift of a pure child."

Jibrīl calmed her fears and suspicions saying, "I am only the messenger of your Lord to give you the gift of a pure child." He's explaining to her that he is not here to harm her in any way, shape, or form. Rather, he has come to her as a messenger of her Lord, sent to give her a gift of good news of a pure boy. The word "pure" here is understood to refer to the fact that her child would be pure and free of any sins. Also, that he would grow up in an environment of purity and goodness.

This response caught Maryam completely off guard. It literally

32 Ibn al-Qayyim, *Badāʾiʿ al-Fawāʾid*, 2:703-4

shocked her and rightfully so. She was shocked for multiple reasons; she had multiple emotions and thoughts running through her mind. How is it possible? How is it going to happen? Why? What will people say?

VERSE 20

قَالَتْ أَنَّىٰ يَكُونُ لِى غُلَٰمٌ وَلَمْ يَمْسَسْنِى بَشَرٌ وَلَمْ أَكُ بَغِيًّا

She said, "How can I have a boy while no man has touched me and I have not been unchaste?"

Maryam عليها السلام is asking how this is possible. "How can I have a son when no man has touched me and I have not been unchaste?" No man has ever touched me before lawfully or unlawfully, through marriage or through illicit means. She's saying, how can she give birth to a child and have a son when she's not even married and it's unimaginable that she would do something wrong. The Quran is alluding to intimate relations but doesn't mention it explicitly. This teaches us the etiquette we should have when discussing private and intimate issues. The word baghī is a name for a woman involved in illicit relationships.

This is somewhat similar to the shock and amazement of Zakariyyā عليه السلام that was mentioned before. The difference between this and the statement of Zakariyyā عليه السلام is that Zakariyyā عليه السلام had asked for a child and was expecting it. Here, Maryam عليها السلام had not even thought about having a child and perhaps her mind raced towards what some of the consequences would be. She was aware of all the potential harms it would bring her and her family if she becomes pregnant. Jibrīl عليه السلام answered her as follows:

VERSE 21

قَـالَ كَذَلِـكِ قَالَ رَبُّـكِ هُـوَ عَلَيَّ هَـيِّنٌ وَلِنَجْعَلَـهُۥ ءَايَـةً لِّلنَّـاسِ
وَرَحْـمَـةً مِّنَّـا ۚ وَكَانَ أَمْـرًا مَّقْضِيًّـا

He said, "Thus [it will be]; your Lord says, 'It is easy for Me,
and We will make him a sign to the people and a mercy
from Us. And it is a matter [already] decreed.'"

J ibrīl responded to her question saying, "Thus [it will be]." Meaning,
you will give birth to a child without marriage and without committing
sin. You will give birth to a child miraculously through the might and
power of Allah according to His divine decree and wisdom. "Your Lord
says, 'It is easy for Me.'" Allah is saying that to create a child from a single
mother without a father is not something difficult or impossible. Why would
it be difficult when Allah has already created a person - the father of humanity Adam - without a mother and a father? Why would it be difficult
when he created a person - Ḥawwā' - from just a male? Why would it be difficult when He created the overwhelming majority of mankind from a male
and a female? It is extremely easy for the One Who when He intends to create
something simply says "Be" and it is.

Allah then mentions two reasons for the miraculous birth of 'Isā .
"We will make him a sign for the people." The word āyah means a sign, proof,
or evidence. His miraculous birth and prophethood will be a sign and proof
of the ultimate might and power of the Lord and Creator of all humanity. It
will serve as a miracle for people to recognize the existence and power of Allah . "And a mercy from Us." Meaning, this child will be a source of mercy
for all of humanity. He will be a Prophet among the Prophets of God calling

towards the oneness and worship of Allah ﷻ that will lead people towards salvation and everlasting felicity. "And it is a matter [already] decreed." Allah ﷻ has already decided that this will happen and now it's going to happen no matter what. It is the will and decree of Allah ﷻ.

VERSE 22

فَحَمَلَتْهُ فَٱنتَبَذَتْ بِهِۦ مَكَانًا قَصِيًّا

So she conceived him, and she withdrew with him to a remote place.

Maryam ؑ accepted the decree of Allah ﷻ, and according to narrations, Jibrīl ؑ blew down her collar and she miraculously conceived. "She withdrew with him to a remote place." This word for withdrawing, intabadhat, was used before when she secluded herself from her family to worship Allah ﷻ. Here she's secluding herself with her unborn child out of a sense of decency and modesty. She went somewhere far away, where people couldn't see her or interact with her so that neither she nor her family would have to hear people gossip and spread rumors about her. Her piety and modesty are extremely important. She comes from a very religious, moral, God-conscious, and important family. She herself was dedicated from birth to worship and she was under the care of a Prophet.

Narrations mention that she went to Bethlehem, which is located in modern day Palestine. One of the lessons or signs of this miraculous birth is to point us towards the ultimate power of Allah ﷻ. To help our limited intellect get an idea of the unlimited power of Allah ﷻ and to really understand the concept of divinity.

According to a few narrations, Maryam 🕊 was engaged to a man named Yūsuf al-Najjār (the Carpenter). al-Rāzī 🕊 narrates a conversation that took place between them. When she conceived he asked Maryam 🕊, "Tell me, do crops grow without seeds? Does a tree grow without rain? Can there be a child without a man?" She replied, "Yes. Don't you know that Allah 🕊 caused crops to grow the day He created them without seeds? And the seeds came from the crops he caused to grow without them. Don't you know that Allah 🕊 created the tree without rain, then through His power made rain a source of life for the tree after having created both of them individually? Or do you say that Allah 🕊 can't cause a tree to grow without the help of rain and if it wasn't for that there would be no tree?" Yūsuf replied, "I don't say that. But I say indeed Allah 🕊 has power over whatever He wills so He says be and it is." Maryam 🕊 then said, "Don't you know that Allah 🕊 created Adam and his wife without a man or woman?"[33] From here Allah 🕊 now mentions the birth of 'Isa 🕊.

VERSE 23

فَأَجَآءَهَا ٱلْمَخَاضُ إِلَىٰ جِذْعِ ٱلنَّخْلَةِ قَالَتْ يَٰلَيْتَنِى مِتُّ قَبْلَ هَٰذَا وَكُنتُ نَسْيًا مَّنسِيًّا

Then the pains of childbirth drove her to the trunk of a palm tree. She said, "Oh, I wish I had died before this and was long forgotten."

---

33   al-Rāzī, *Tafsīr al-Rāzī*, 21:201-202

Meaning, the pains of childbirth, her contractions, and all of the difficulties she was experiencing forced her to seek physical support from the trunk of a date palm. She leaned against the trunk of the date palm or held on to it in order to relieve some of the physical pain she was experiencing. This is a very vivid and powerful description of how Maryam was feeling. The pains of childbirth, the pain felt by a mother when giving birth, her contractions, are indescribable. Anyone with children, particularly mothers, knows how painful and difficult this process is. She was also experiencing emotional pain as well as understood from the previous verse.

The culmination of all of this physical and emotional pain caused her to say, "Oh, I wish I had died before this and was long forgotten." I wish I could have been taken from the life of this world before all of this pain and difficulty and before people would accuse me and question my modesty, chastity, and morality. I wish that I could die before people accuse me of this sin and look down upon my family and me. This is an extremely powerful expression that captures her feelings and emotions. This is how important modesty, honor, and chastity were to her. She'd rather be dead than be accused of illicit relations and have that as a stain on her and her family. "And was long forgotten." Meaning, not only dead but completely forgotten and erased from people's memories. Immediately after expressing her deep emotions and exposing her vulnerability before Allah , He sent His unique and infinite mercy upon her.

VERSE 24

فَنَادَىٰهَا مِن تَحْتِهَآ أَلَّا تَحْزَنِي قَدْ جَعَلَ رَبُّكِ تَحْتَكِ سَرِيًّا

So he called her from below her, "Do not grieve! Your Lord has provided a stream at your feet.

"So he called out from below her, 'Do not grieve.'" Meaning, someone called out from below her telling her not to be worried, grieved, anxious, or sad. The scholars of tafsīr mention two different explanations here. The first is that Jibrīl ﷺ called out to her consoling and comforting her; telling her not to be sad. The second is that Allah ﷻ allowed ʿIsā ﷺ to miraculously speak at that moment comforting his mother and telling her not to be sad. "Your Lord has provided a stream at your feet." Allah ﷻ caused a small stream to flow at her feet so she could drink water, quench her thirst, cool off, and wash up.

VERSE 25

وَهُزِّىٓ إِلَيْكِ بِجِذْعِ ٱلنَّخْلَةِ تُسَٰقِطْ عَلَيْكِ رُطَبًا جَنِيًّا

And shake the trunk of this palm tree towards you, it will drop fresh, ripe dates upon you.

As another sign that everything will be alright, that the help and mercy of Allah ﷻ are with her, as a source of comfort, reassurance, and consolation, she was told to shake the trunk of the date palm that she was leaning against and getting support from. Once she shook the trunk, the date palm would drop fresh, ripe dates upon her. It's mentioned in a few narrations that this particular date palm was dry, devoid of fruit and fonds and was in the middle of the desert. However, when she shook the trunk, fresh ripe dates miraculously fell upon her.

Here it is important to note that according to the majority of scholars, Maryam ﷺ is not considered to be a prophet. However, we find that Allah ﷻ used her to display several miraculous things as a sign of His infinite might and power. Generally speaking, in English, all unusual and supernatural events are referred to as miracles. However, within our Sharīʿah and system of belief we differentiate between different types of "miracles." The Arabic language marks the subtle differences that exist between each type. A miracle, muʿjizah, is an unusual event that occurs at the hands of a prophet but is purely an act of Allah ﷻ; the prophet has no role in its creation whatsoever. A miracle is defined as "a clear interruption in God's normal pattern of creating things - one that is inimitable (such that no other can perform the like) and is granted to someone who claims to be a prophet sent by God, the exalted."[34] In other words, a miracle is a divine act that defies and transcends universal norms and laws, which Allah ﷻ grants to His prophets and messengers in order to convince people of the truth of their message.

A saintly[35] miracle, or karāmah, is also something extraordinary. It's an act of Allah ﷻ but it appears at the hands of someone close to Allah ﷻ. It is an "act of God ﷻ that contradicts His customary norm, with the consequence that the servant realizes the fruit of his worship, and [as a result], his insight regarding the validity of his religion may increase."[36] This incident of ripe dates falling on her lap after shaking a dry barren tree and a stream flowing at her feet are classified as saintly miracles.

Another interesting point to note is that If Allah ﷻ had willed, He could have caused the dates to fall in her lap without having her shake the tree. Allah ﷻ commanded her to shake the tree to show how important it is to use the means that we have available to us. The amount of sustenance, food,

34 Khan, *An Introduction to Islamic Theology*, 116

35 According to theologians, a saint (walī) is defined as "one who knows God and His attributes, based on human capacity; who is consistent in obedience and avoids disobedience, meaning not that he never commits a wrong, for he is not infallible like prophets, but that he does not sin without repenting from it; and who turns away from indulgence in even lawful pleasures and desires, although he may still partake of them, especially with an intention to gain strength for worship." (taken from Sh. Faraz Khan's excellent end notes of Imam Nūr al-Dīn al-Ṣābūnī's *al-Bidāyah fī Uṣūl al-Dīn*, p. 208-209 endnote 42) Allah ﷻ defines the awliyā' as "those who are faithful and are mindful ⌜of Him⌝. For them is good news in this worldly life and the Hereafter. There is no change in the promise of Allah. That is ⌜truly⌝ the ultimate triumph." (10:63-64)

36 Khan, *An Introduction to Islamic Theology*, 182

drink, and water each of us is going to receive throughout our lives has already been determined and decreed by Allah ﷻ. However, that doesn't mean that we will receive our sustenance automatically without any effort; money, food, drink, and clothes will not just fall into our laps. We still have to work hard and strive for it using all of the available resources at our disposal. Planning, preparing, and putting forth our best efforts is not contrary to the concept of yaqīn (certainty in Allah's promise) or tawakkul, having trust in Allah ﷻ. All of this is an essential aspect of placing our absolute trust in Allah ﷻ. Allah ﷻ then tells Maryam عليها السلام to eat, drink, and clear her mind. He's ﷻ telling her to not worry about what is going to be said about her and what she'll be accused of.

VERSE 26

فَكُلِي وَٱشْرَبِي وَقَرِّي عَيْنًا ۖ فَإِمَّا تَرَيِنَّ مِنَ ٱلْبَشَرِ أَحَدًا فَقُولِيٓ إِنِّي
نَذَرْتُ لِلرَّحْمَٰنِ صَوْمًا فَلَنْ أُكَلِّمَ ٱلْيَوْمَ إِنسِيًّا

So eat and drink and cool your eyes. And if you see any human being, say, 'Indeed, I have vowed to the Lord of Mercy to abstain from conversation, and I will not talk to anyone today.'

Allah ﷻ is continuing to console, comfort, and reassure Maryam عليها السلام telling her to eat the dates, drink the water from the spring, be content, and relax. "Cool your eyes" is an Arabic expression used for happiness, joy, and contentment. Satiating your hunger and thirst along with looking after your newborn child will bring contentment to your heart;

it will cause all your worries and concerns to melt away. Parents, especially mothers, find comfort in looking at their children with love and tenderness.

Allah ﷻ then instructs her not to engage anyone in conversation. "And if you see any human being, say, 'Indeed, I have vowed to the Lord of Mercy to abstain from conversation, and I will not talk to anyone today.'" Allah ﷻ knew that if someone were to see her with a child they would become nosy and start asking all types of questions. In response, Maryam ﷺ would have to respond and defend herself and her honor. To save her from that difficulty and unnecessary stress, Allah ﷻ instructed her to take a vow of silence. There is no need for her to explain herself to anyone.

On a side note, keeping a vow of silence as an act of worship was something that existed in previous religions and has been abrogated in Islam. Once the Prophet ﷺ saw a man standing in the sun and asked, "What's wrong with him?" They said, "He has taken a vow not to speak, nor to seek shade from the sun, nor to sit and to fast." So the Prophet ﷺ said, "Tell him to speak, seek shade, sit and complete his fast."[37] Another narration mentions that Abū Bakr ؓ ran into a woman who took a vow of silence so he told her, "Islam has abolished this as an act of worship so speak." The purpose of worship in Islam is to purify oneself and to gain righteousness. Any difficulty that is found in these acts is to reach these high goals. Worship is not a type of punishment so to go through unnecessary hardship is something that is not part of our religion.

Within Islam, we are supposed to refrain from sinful speech while fasting such as cursing, lying, and backbiting. The Prophet ﷺ said, "Fasting is a protection for you, so when you are fasting, do not behave obscenely or foolishly, and if any one argues with you or abuses you, say, 'I am fasting. I am fasting.'"[38] The Prophet ﷺ also said, "Whoever does not leave false speech, and acting according to it, then Allah is not in any need of him leaving his food and his drink."[39]

Maryam ﷺ witnessed and experienced the infinite mercy of Allah ﷻ and saw that the help of Allah ﷻ was with her. After passing through her 40 days of postnatal bleeding she returned to her people with ʿIsā ﷺ.

---

37 Bukhārī, *k. al-aymān wa al-nudhūr, b. al-nadhr fī mā la yamlik wa fī maʿṣiyyah*, 6704

38 Mālik, *k. al-ṣiyām*, 690

39 Bukhārī, *k. al-ṣawm, b. Man lam yadaʿ qawl al-zūr wa al-ʿamal bihi fī al-ṣawm*, 1903

VERSE 27

فَأَتَتْ بِهِۦ قَوْمَهَا تَحْمِلُهُۥ ۖ قَالُوا۟ يَـٰمَرْيَمُ لَقَدْ جِئْتِ شَيْـًٔا فَرِيًّا

Then she returned to her people, carrying him. They said, "O Maryam, you have certainly done a terrible thing.

After being comforted by the infinite mercy and grace of Allah ﷻ and after she was reassured that Allah ﷻ would protect her from being dishonored and disgraced, she returned with the newborn baby to her hometown. As a result of these immense favors and blessings from Allah ﷻ, she fully submitted to Allah's decree and returned with pride and full confidence. She wasn't embarrassed or ashamed and she wasn't trying to hide the baby. She knew that Allah ﷻ would defend and protect her honor. As soon as her people saw her with a child they started with the accusations. They said, "O Maryam, you have certainly done a terrible thing."

The word "fariyy" literally means to cut or to split and is used to describe a task that involves a lot of cutting and chopping. Here it means something grave, strange, and unexpected; something that is extremely disliked and looked down upon. You have come with a newborn child without having been married. How could you have done something so shameful when you come from such an upright family?

يَـٰٓأُخْتَ هَـٰرُونَ مَا كَانَ أَبُوكِ ٱمْرَأَ سَوْءٍ وَمَا كَانَتْ أُمُّكِ بَغِيًّا

O sister of Hārūn! Your father was not an evil man, nor
was your mother unchaste."

"O sister of Hārūn!" Hārūn 🕮, Musa's 🕮 brother and companion, had passed away centuries before the time of Maryam
🕮. That is why the commentators mention that this expres-
sion is not supposed to be understood literally. They mention a few possible
explanations:

1. She was from the descendants of Hārūn 🕮 and it was customary to
   associate people with their ancestors.
2. Others mention that she actually had a brother named Hārūn who
   was named after the Prophet. It was customary, and still is, to name
   children after historical or religious figures.
3. Others say it is the name of a righteous person from her time and
   she is being called his sister because she was also known for her righteousness and piety.

They're invoking the name of Hārūn to show the gravity of what they're
accusing her of. How could you tarnish that name by bringing it shame and
disgrace? "Your father was not an evil man." The word "saw'" literally means
evil, someone who openly commits sin. So they were indicating that her father was a righteous and pious man. "Nor was your mother unchaste". Your
mother was a woman of modesty and honor known for her chastity. In simple words, they are accusing her of committing a grave sin while rebuking

and reprimanding her at the same time. How can you, a woman who comes from such a good and noble family, do such a thing? This is totally unexpected from you.

Generally speaking, when someone accuses you in public and slanders you, and then on top of that brings your family into it, you become angry, upset, and respond. However, Maryam 🕌 remained patient relying upon the promise of Allah 🕌 and simply pointed towards 'Isā 🕌.

VERSE 29

فَأَشَارَتْ إِلَيْهِ ۖ قَالُوا كَيْفَ نُكَلِّمُ مَن كَانَ فِي ٱلْمَهْدِ صَبِيًّا

So she pointed to him. They said, "How can we speak to one who is still a child in the cradle?"

Instead of responding to their accusations and slander she pointed to 'Isā 🕌 indicating to them to get their answers from him. They were caught off guard, shocked, surprised, and offended by this response. They were asking her a very serious question and she replied by pointing to the newborn. They responded sarcastically with a rhetorical question saying, "How can we speak to one who is still a child in the cradle?" It is not possible for a newborn to speak and you know that very well. Allah 🕌 then miraculously granted 'Isā 🕌 the ability to speak from the lap of his mother. He declared the innocence, chastity, and purity of his mother and described himself with nine qualities and characteristics.

VERSE 30

قَالَ إِنِّى عَبْدُ ٱللَّهِ ءَاتَىٰنِىَ ٱلْكِتَـٰبَ وَجَعَلَنِى نَبِيًّا

He [ʿIsā ﷺ] said, "Truly I am a servant of Allah. He has given me the Scripture and made me a prophet.

ʿIsā ﷺ opened his statement in a very simple yet powerful and emphatic manner declaring, "Truly I am a servant of Allah." I am a slave and servant of Allah ﷻ dedicated to His service and worship alone. He is highlighting the nature of the relationship between him and Allah ﷻ; Allah ﷻ is his Lord and Master and he is His servant and slave. With this one simple statement he made it absolutely clear that, although he was born miraculously without a father, he was still a human being. This is an indirect refutation of those Christians who believe in the divinity of ʿIsā ﷺ. Allah ﷻ knew that some Christians would claim that he's God or the son of God. He is clarifying that there is nothing divine about him. In reality, he is a servant of the Divine.

ʿIsā ﷺ continued, "He has given me the Scripture." Meaning, Allah ﷻ will give me the Injīl (Bible) as a book of guidance for my people. The past tense is used to talk about something that will happen in the future to convey the meaning of certainty. It will happen without a doubt.

"And made me a prophet." Meaning, Allah ﷻ will make him a prophet at the appropriate time. Again, the past tense is used to describe something that will happen in the future to convey the meaning of certainty, which is a common literary technique used in the Quran. The meaning being conveyed is that Allah ﷻ will definitely make him a prophet.

VERSE 31

وَجَعَلَنِي مُبَارَكًا أَيْنَ مَا كُنتُ وَأَوْصَٰنِي بِٱلصَّلَوٰةِ وَٱلزَّكَوٰةِ مَا دُمْتُ حَيًّا

And He has made me blessed wherever I may be and has enjoined prayer and zakāh upon me as long as I am alive.

The fourth quality that ʿIsā ﷺ describes himself with is, "And He has made me blessed wherever I may be." Not only will he be chosen and selected as a prophet with revelation, but he will also be a source of blessings wherever he may be. He will always bring benefit and ease to people by teaching them right from wrong, good character, morality, and guiding them towards the truth. Not only will he be blessed himself, but he will also be a source of blessings for others. He was sent with mercy to the Children of Israel to make their law easier upon them. It's said that as a result of his blessings, whenever ignorant, ill-mannered people interacted with him they miraculously became wise and well-mannered.

ʿIsā ﷺ then mentions the fifth quality saying, "And has enjoined prayer and zakāh upon me as long as I am alive." The use of the word "awṣā" means that Allah ﷻ has firmly commanded him to. It's derived from the word "waṣiyah," which means to bequeath. When used in the context of issuing an order it implies an emphatic command. He's saying that Allah ﷻ has commanded him to remain steadfast upon prayer and charity as long as he is alive and able to do so.

These two acts of worship, ṣalāh and zakāh, were prescribed in the laws of all previous prophets and messengers. However, their details were different in each religion, but the purpose, objective, and wisdom behind them was the same. All ritual acts of worship have higher aims and objectives behind them. Prayer connects an individual with their Creator and prevents them from sin. Zakāh and charity purify one's wealth and soul and serve as financial assistance for the weak and poor.

VERSE 32

وَبَرًّا بِوَٰلِدَتِي وَلَمْ يَجْعَلْنِي جَبَّارًا شَقِيًّا

And [He has made me] dutiful to my mother, and He has not made me arrogant or wretched.

ʿIsā ﷷ continues describing himself saying, "And [He has made me] dutiful to my mother." The word "barr" means righteous, dutiful, obedient, and respectful. As mentioned earlier, it gives the meaning of being obedient, loving, respectful, and dutiful to one's parents. Birr al-Wālidayn (righteousness with one's parents) includes serving one's parents, listening to them, taking care of them, dealing with them with humility, gentleness, compassion, and care, showing them honor, and fulfilling their needs and necessities. It can be understood as general good conduct towards one's parents. ʿIsā ﷷ was obedient and respectful to his mother. A very unique point here is that he only mentions his mother, highlighting that his birth was miraculous. This has been highlighted because of its importance and also because this is something that had become very uncommon among the Children of Israel just as it has in today's modern world.

"And He has not made me arrogant or wretched." The word "jabbār" refers to a person who has pride and arrogance; one who thinks they're better than everyone else. ʿIsā ﷷ was a man of humility; he was not arrogant, prideful, or disobedient. He was the opposite; gentle, humble, and obedient. "Shaqiyy," unfortunate, is the opposite of "saʿīd," fortunate. It is usually used to describe a person who is unfortunate and wretched because of their sins, arrogance, pride, and disobedience. ʿIsā ﷺ is describing himself as a person of humility, dignity, and respect and as a person who is fortunate. Humility and fortune go together. On the other hand, a person who is arrogant will be wretched in this world and the next.

VERSE 33

وَٱلسَّلَـٰمُ عَلَىَّ يَوْمَ وُلِدتُّ وَيَوْمَ أَمُوتُ وَيَوْمَ أُبْعَثُ حَيًّا

And safety and security are upon me the day I was born and the day I will die and the day I am raised alive.

This is very similar to how Allah ﷻ describes Yaḥyā ﷺ in verse 15. ʿIsā ﷺ is telling them that there was salām - safety, security, refuge, and blessings - upon him the day he was born, there will be salām upon him the day he passes away, and the day he is resurrected. In other words, he's under the protection, care, guidance, and security of Allah ﷻ throughout his life. This statement is also an indirect proof against the Christians. He's explicitly saying that he's a servant of Allah ﷻ just like every other human that was born, will die, and be resurrected. What's interesting, according to some commentators of the Quran, is that this same passage was part of the Injīl, but was later distorted and changed.

ذَٰلِكَ عِيسَى ٱبْنُ مَرْيَمَ قَوْلَ ٱلْحَقِّ ٱلَّذِى فِيهِ يَمْتَرُونَ

That is 'Isā, the son of Maryam - [This is] a word of truth about which they are in doubt.

"**D**hālik" is a demonstrative pronoun in the Arabic language that is used to indicate or gesture towards something that is in the distance. It is usually translated as "that." Here, it's referring to the description of 'Isā 🕊 mentioned in the last few verses. Meaning, the person who was just described as the slave of Allah 🕊, a prophet who will be given scripture, someone who is blessed and a source of blessings is 'Isā 🕊 the son of Maryam 🕊. "[This is] a word of truth about which they are in doubt." The next word, "qawl," has been read in two ways; it can be recited with a ḍammah or a fatḥah on the final letter. If it's recited with a ḍammah the meaning being conveyed is that 'Isā 🕊 is the word of truth. The entire expression will be a title for 'Isā 🕊, just as he has been given the title 'the Word of Allah'. If it's recited with a fatḥah, then the meaning is that these words that have just been recited are the absolute truth; there's no doubt or confusion about them whatsoever.

"About which they are in doubt." The Jews and Christians had beliefs about 'Isā 🕊 that were based on doubts and falsehood. The Christians revered and exalted him to such a level of reverence that they took him as the son of God; they attribute qualities of divinity to him. The Jews, on the other hand, denigrated him maliciously and called him, God forbid, an illegitimate child.

In these verses, Allah 🕊 clarifies the correct belief regarding 'Isā 🕊 highlighting that he is a slave of Allah 🕊 who has been selected and chosen as a prophet. Allah ﷻ then explicitly rejects the claim of the Christians that ʿIsā ﷺ is the son of God.

VERSE 35

مَا كَانَ لِلَّهِ أَن يَتَّخِذَ مِن وَلَدٍۖ سُبْحَـٰنَهُۥٓۚ إِذَا قَضَىٰٓ أَمْرًا فَإِنَّمَا
يَقُولُ لَهُۥ كُن فَيَكُونُ

It is not [befitting] for Allah to take a son; exalted is He! When He decrees a matter, He only says, "Be," and it is.

This verse is a declaration of the oneness, greatness, might, power, and magnificence of Allah ﷻ. It is not befitting, appropriate, or even logical for Allah ﷻ to have a son. Allah ﷻ is absolutely unique and independent. He does not need or require companionship in the form of a spouse, children, or family. Allah ﷻ is the Divine, the Creator, and having children is from the characteristics of His creation. There's no resemblance, similarity, or comparison between Allah ﷻ and His creation. The Creator is ever-living, eternal, and free of all need. "Exalted is He!" Allah ﷻ is exalted and far above from having or wanting a son. Oftentimes, the expression "subḥānAllah" is translated as "glory be to Allah" or "Allah is exalted". It conveys the meaning of Allah's ﷻ absolute perfection. Allah ﷻ is free from any deficiencies, faults, blemishes, and shortcomings. It's a statement that declares the perfection of Allah ﷻ by negating all imperfections, which gives us a slight understanding of Allah's divinity. Allah ﷻ is far above and sanctified from what they ascribe to Him. It helps us understand that Allah ﷻ is beyond human comprehension.

Allah ﷻ concludes the verse by highlighting His infinite might and power. "When He decrees a matter, He only says, 'Be,' and it is." The miraculous birth of ʿIsā ﷺ is part of the divine decree of Allah ﷻ. It is not a proof of ʿIsā's ﷺ divinity or being the son of God. Rather, it's the decree of Allah ﷻ, and His ﷻ decree is such that when He wants to create something He says, "Be!" and it is. How can a Being that has such power have, want, or need a child? If you believe that the birth of ʿIsā ﷺ is miraculous and all the things he did were miraculous, then think and reflect over the power of the One who caused those miracles to happen. Allah ﷻ then mentions one more statement that ʿIsā ﷺ made to his people.

VERSE 36

وَإِنَّ ٱللَّهَ رَبِّى وَرَبُّكُمْ فَٱعْبُدُوهُ ۚ هَٰذَا صِرَٰطٌ مُّسْتَقِيمٌ

[ʿIsā ﷺ said], 'And truly Allah is my Lord and your Lord, so worship Him. This is a straight path."

The previous two verses were statements of Allah ﷻ. Here Allah ﷻ continues to relate what ʿIsā ﷺ said to those who accused his mother of indecency. "And truly Allah is my Lord and your Lord, so worship Him." Allah ﷻ is the Lord of the universe and every single thing it contains so worship Him alone without any partners. The word "rabb" is a very unique and comprehensive word. It has multiple layers of meaning; it refers to the one who creates, maintains, sustains, provides, nurtures, protects, and guides. A "rabb" is someone who creates something then takes care of it. Allah ﷻ alone is our Lord so "worship Him" alone without any partners.

Worshipping Allah ﷻ alone through submission, devotion, obedience, and servitude is the Straight Path. The Straight Path is referring to the way of life of Islam, the divinely revealed set of beliefs and practices that lead a person towards success in this life and salvation in the Hereafter. Islam, the holisitc way of life that has been revealed by Allah ﷻ is the one and only true path to salvation. This is the belief and way of life that will lead one to guidance and eternal happiness. Whoever follows something else will be misled.

Despite the fact that Allah ﷻ clarified the truth regarding ʿIsā عليه السلام, that he is the servant of Allah ﷻ and a prophet, the Christians still had disagreements regarding him. Is he God? The son of God? The holy spirit? Is he all three in one?

VERSE 37

فَٱخْتَلَفَ ٱلْأَحْزَابُ مِنۢ بَيْنِهِمْ ۖ فَوَيْلٌ لِّلَّذِينَ كَفَرُوا۟ مِن مَّشْهَدِ
يَوْمٍ عَظِيمٍ

Then the groups among them fell in dispute. So, how evil is the fate of the disbelievers when they have to face the Great Day.

In this verse, Allah ﷻ is referring to the disagreement different groups and sects from the People of the Book had regarding ʿIsā عليه السلام. Some of the Jews claimed that he was - and we seek refuge with Allah ﷻ from such ill thoughts - an illegitimate child. The various groups, sects, and denominations of the Christians disagree among themselves regarding the reality of ʿIsā عليه السلام. Some claim he is God, others say he's the son of God, others say he's the holy spirit, and others say he's all three in one.

"So, how evil is the fate of the disbelievers when they have to face the Great Day." This is a severe warning and threat to those who fabricate lies against Allah ﷻ and speak about Him without knowledge or proof. The word "wayl" means severe punishment, destruction, or it could also be the name of a valley in Hellfire. These various groups that made false claims and held false beliefs about ʿIsā عليه السلام will have severe punishment, destruction, and a place in Hellfire on the tremendous day, which is the Day of Judgment.

Despite the gravity of their false claims, beliefs, and lies, Allah ﷻ allows them to live in this world and enjoy His blessings and favors; He ﷻ gives them the opportunity to change or allows them to dig a deeper hole for themselves. As the Prophet ﷺ said, "There is no one more patient than Allah ﷻ with harmful words. They attribute a son to Him yet He still provides for them and gives them heath."[40] Allah ﷻ tells us in Sūrah Ibrāhīm, "Do not think [O Prophet] that Allah is unaware of what the wrongdoers do. He only delays them until a Day when [their] eyes will stare in horror."[41]

Allah ﷻ then tells us how sharp their senses of hearing and seeing will be on the Day of Judgment as opposed to their inability to hear or see the truth in this world.

VERSE 38

أَسْمِعْ بِهِمْ وَأَبْصِرْ يَوْمَ يَأْتُونَنَا ۖ لَٰكِنِ ٱلظَّٰلِمُونَ ٱلْيَوْمَ فِى ضَلَٰلٍ مُّبِينٍ

40 Bukhārī, *k. al-tawḥīd, b. qawl Allah taʿāla [inna Allah huwa al-razzāq dhū al-quwwah al-matīn]*, 7378

41 وَلَا تَحْسَبَنَّ اللَّهَ غَافِلًا عَمَّا يَعْمَلُ الظَّالِمُونَ ۚ إِنَّمَا يُؤَخِّرُهُمْ لِيَوْمٍ تَشْخَصُ فِيهِ الْأَبْصَارُ - 14:42

How clearly will they hear and see on the Day they will come to Us! But today the wrongdoers are clearly astray.

The opening verbs of this verse are on a verb pattern known as afʿāl al-taʿajjub, verbs of amazement. They are verbs that express astonishment and surprise. How amazing and strong is their ability to hear now that they have come to us on the Day of Judgment! How amazing and powerful is their sight now that they can see the truth! They have no trouble hearing or seeing now that they have come for judgment and recompense. Whereas, in the life of this world they were deaf and blind to the truth. They have ears, there's absolutely nothing wrong with their faculty of hearing, but they are unable to understand the truth and reality of what is being said to them. They are unable to process the teachings, guidance, and warnings of the prophets and messengers. They have eyes with which they can't see. Again, there's nothing wrong with their faculty of sight, but they are unable to recognize the truth that is right in front of them. There's something wrong with their ability to process the information they hear and see. That's why Allah ﷻ describes them as the wrongdoers who are in open error. "But today the wrongdoers are clearly astray." The word "ẓālimūn" literally means those who put something in its improper place. It is used to refer to those who disobey Allah ﷻ and disbelieve. They are unjust and wrong in their beliefs and false claims regarding ʿIsā عليه السلام. Allah ﷻ then tells the Prophet ﷺ to warn them.

VERSE 39

وَأَنذِرْهُمْ يَوْمَ ٱلْحَسْرَةِ إِذْ قُضِىَ ٱلْأَمْرُ وَهُمْ فِى غَفْلَةٍ وَهُمْ لَا يُؤْمِنُونَ

And warn them, [O Muḥammad], of the Day of Regret, when the matter will be settled, while they are heedless and do not believe.

"And warn them [O Muḥammad] about the Day of Regret." One of the responsibilities of the Prophet ﷺ was to warn against disbelief, acts of disobedience, and immorality. One of the titles given to the Prophet ﷺ is al-Nadhīr, the Warner, which refers to one who warns with genuine care and concern. Allah ﷻ is telling the Prophet ﷺ to warn both the non-believers and the believers, give them a heads up, regarding the Day of Regret. The word used here for regret is "ḥasrah," which isn't the normal feeling of regret or remorse. Rather it's severe regret, remorse, and sorrow that leads to sadness.

The Day of Judgment has been described with several different names and titles that describe and capture various aspects of that fearful day. Here, Allah ﷻ refers to it as the Day of Regret because on that day every single human being will have some type of regret and remorse. Those who were righteous believers will feel a sense of regret and remorse for not having done more. They will have this desire to go back to the world so that they could engage in more acts of worship and remembrance of Allah ﷻ. They will want to return to this life so that they could just say one more subḥānAllah or alḥamdulillāh. As Mu'adh ؓ narrated the Prophet ﷺ said, "The people of paradise will regret only one thing, namely those moments that were spent without the remembrance of Allah."[42]

On the other hand, those who disbelieved and sinned will regret the choices they made in the life of this world. They will regret their arrogance, pride, and rejection of the truth. They will regret living a life of misguidance, sin, and disobedience. Allah ﷻ describes the reason for their remorse and regret saying, "While they are heedless and do not believe." They are totally heedless and careless regarding the nature and reality of this world and the next. They refuse to believe in life after death because of their pride, arrogance, and ignorance. They're enjoying the life of this world and get so caught up in its pleasures, luxuries, and comforts that they forget about the life to come. They forget that this life is temporary and that the next is eter-

42 al-Bayhaqī, *Shuʿab al-Īmān*, #508-510 2:54-6 and al-Ṭabarānī, *al-Muʿjam al-Kabīr*, 20:93

nal.

There are many factors that lead towards "ghaflah." However, the underlying cause is the failure to recognize the reality of this life. They fail to realize that the life of this world is temporary and fleeting; that it is eventually going to come to an end and that the life of the Hereafter is forever. That's why people waste so much time, energy, and effort chasing after things that are temporary and fleeting. As al-Ḥasan al-Baṣrī ◈ said, "Love of the world is the origin of every sin."[43] The root cause of every single sin or act of disobedience a person commits is love of this world.

Abū Saʿīd al-Khudrī ◈ narrated that the Messenger of Allah ◈ said, "When the people of Paradise enter Paradise and the people of Fire the Fire, death will be brought in the form of a striped ram. It will be made to stop in between Paradise and Hell. It will then be said, 'Oh people of Paradise do you know what this is?' They will look at it and examine it and say, 'Yes, this is death.' Then the command will be passed and it will be slaughtered. Then it will be said, 'Oh people of Paradise, eternity without death and O people of Hell, eternity without death.' Then the Prophet ◈ recited 'And warn them, [O Muḥammad], of the Day of Regret, when the matter will be settled, while they are heedless and do not believe.' Then he said, 'The people of this world are lost in this world.'"[44]

VERSE 40

إِنَّا نَحْنُ نَرِثُ ٱلْأَرْضَ وَمَنْ عَلَيْهَا وَإِلَيْنَا يُرْجَعُونَ

43 al-Suyūṭī, *Tadrīb al-Rāwī*, 1: 486

44 Muslim, *k. al-jannah wa ṣifah naʿīmihā wa ahlihā, b. al-nār yadkhuluhā al-jabbārun wa al-jannah yadkhuluhā al-ḍuʿafā,* 2849

Indeed, it is We who will inherit the earth and whoever is on it, and to Us they will be returned.

This verse is similar to an endnote or a conclusion; it serves as a conclusion for the entire passage. Allah ﷻ is reminding us that He ﷻ alone is the One who remains and is everlasting. He ﷻ inherits the earth and whoever is on it in the sense that every single thing will cease to exist, except for Him. He ﷻ alone is the Master and Owner of everything. On the Day of Judgment every human will be brought and gathered before Allah ﷻ for judgment, accountability, and recompense.

LESSONS AND BENEFITS FROM THE STORY OF MARYAM عليها السلام AND ʿISĀ عليه السلام

1.

Seclusion - The world is full of several distractions that are constantly competing for our attention. Allah ﷻ tells us, "The enjoyment of [worldly] desires—women, children, treasures of gold and silver, fine horses, cattle, and fertile land—has been made appealing to people. These are the pleasures of this worldly life, but with Allah is the finest destination."[45] All of these distractions take us away from our true purpose in life, which is to worship Allah ﷻ. Sometimes, it's a good idea to disconnect from the world, to remove ourselves from all of these distractions and competing forces, to recenter ourselves and remind ourselves of our real purpose in life. Sometimes we lose focus and need to take a break in order to regain that focus. Perhaps that's one of the reasons why we have iʿtikāf, seclusion in the masjid, as an act of worship.

Iʿtikāf is entering the masjid with the intention to remain there for worship in order to get close to Allah ﷻ. The Mother of the Believers, ʿĀ'ishah رضي الله عنها said, "The Prophet ﷺ would always perform iʿtikāf in the last ten days of

45 3:14 - زُيِّنَ لِلنَّاسِ حُبُّ الشَّهَوَاتِ مِنَ النِّسَاءِ وَالْبَنِينَ وَالْقَنَاطِيرِ الْمُقَنطَرَةِ مِنَ الذَّهَبِ وَالْفِضَّةِ وَالْخَيْلِ الْمُسَوَّمَةِ وَالْأَنْعَامِ وَالْحَرْثِ ۗ ذَٰلِكَ مَتَاعُ الْحَيَاةِ الدُّنْيَا ۖ وَاللَّهُ عِندَهُ حُسْنُ الْمَآبِ

Ramaḍān until Allah Most High took his soul."[46] Ibn al-Qayyim ﷺ writes, "The purpose of iʿtikaf is that the heart gets attached to God, and with it, one attains inner composure and equanimity and preoccupation with the mundane things of life ceases and absorption in the Eternal Reality takes place, and the state is reached in which all fears, hopes and apprehensions are superseded by the love and remembrance of God, every anxiety is transformed into anxiety for Him, and every thought and feeling is blended with the eagerness to gain His nearness and earn His good favor, and devotion to the Almighty is generated instead of devotion to the world and it becomes the provision for the grave where there will be neither a friend nor a helper. This is the high aim and purpose of iʿtikāf which is the specialty of the most sublime part of Ramaḍān, meaning the last 10 days." [47]

2.

Seeking Refuge with Allah ﷻ - From this passage we learn how to protect ourselves from our desires. We learn that whenever we find ourselves in a situation where we may fall prey to our desires, we should seek refuge, safety, and protection with Allah ﷻ. This is the same lesson we learn from the story of Yūsuf ﷺ when he was seduced by the wife of the Minister. Allah ﷻ tells us, "And the lady, in whose house he lived, tried to seduce him. She locked the doors [firmly] and said, 'Come to me!' He replied, 'Allah is my refuge! It is [not right to betray] my master, who has taken good care of me. Indeed, the wrongdoers never succeed.'"[48] The istiʿādhah is a very powerful tool for seeking Allah's help, protection, safety, and refuge.

3.

Protection from Harm - One of the most effective ways of protecting ourselves from harm is by reminding the one who's hurting us about Allah ﷻ. The mention of Allah ﷻ is supposed to have a powerful effect upon the one who says it and the one who hears it. As Allah ﷻ says, "The [true] believers are only those whose hearts tremble at the remembrance of Allah." [49]

46 Muslim, *k. al-iʿtikāf, b. iʿtikāf al-ʿashr al-awākhir min ramaḍān*, 1172

47 ibn al-Qayyim, *Zād al-Maʿād*,

48 وَرَاوَدَتْهُ الَّتِي هُوَ فِي بَيْتِهَا عَن نَّفْسِهِ وَغَلَّقَتِ الْأَبْوَابَ وَقَالَتْ هَيْتَ لَكَ ۚ قَالَ مَعَاذَ اللَّهِ ۖ إِنَّهُ رَبِّي أَحْسَنَ مَثْوَايَ ۖ إِنَّهُ لَا يُفْلِحُ الظَّالِمُونَ - 12:23

49 إِنَّمَا الْمُؤْمِنُونَ الَّذِينَ إِذَا ذُكِرَ اللَّهُ وَجِلَتْ قُلُوبُهُمْ - 8:2

Jābir 🙵 narrates that he accompanied the Messenger of Allah 🙶 on an expedition towards Najd. When the Messenger of Allah 🙶 returned, he returned with him. It was in the afternoon when they reached a valley in which there were many thorny trees. The Messenger of Allah 🙶 dismounted and the people scattered in order to find some shade beneath the trees. The Messenger of Allah 🙶 dismounted beneath an acacia tree and hung his sword on it. We fell asleep for some time and suddenly we heard the Messenger of Allah 🙶 calling us. On reaching him, we saw a bedouin next to him. The Messenger of Allah 🙶 said to us, "This person took my sword while I was sleeping. I woke up and saw the unsheathed sword in his hand. He then said to me, 'Who is going to save you from me?' I replied, 'Allah,' three times."[50] Another version adds, "The sword fell from the man's hand and the Messenger of Allah 🙶 took it and said, 'Who is going to save you from me?' The man replied, 'Be kind when you have power over me.'"[51]

4.

Communal Benefit vs. Individual Benefit - Oftentimes, an individual may be made to go through challenges and hardships for the benefit of the community. In this story, we learn that Maryam 🙴 was made to undergo such great difficulty and emotional pain for the betterment of society. The sacrifice, patience, perseverance, and endurance of one individual can have far reaching effects and outcomes.

5.

Comfort - When a person is going through physical and mental distress, it is important to engage in some sort of coping mechanism. A person should do something that will get their mind off their pain or feelings. Maryam 🙴 was told to eat, drink, and enjoy the company of her newborn to get her mind off her worries and forget about her problems for a short while.

6.

---

50   Bukhārī, k. al-jihād wa al-siyar, b. man ʿallaqa sayfahu bī al-shajar fī al-safar ʿind al-qāʾilah, 2910

51   Aḥmad, Musnad, #14929, 15190, ʿAbd ibn Ḥumayd, Musnad, #1094, and Abū Yaʿlā, Musnad, #1778

Avoid Useless Arguments - From this story, we also learn the importance of avoiding useless arguments and debates. The purpose of an argument, debate, or discussion should be to arrive at the truth. Useless argumentation and debates have been discouraged in the Quran and several statements of the Prophet ﷺ. The Prophet ﷺ said, "No people go astray after having followed right guidance, but those who indulge in disputes." Then he recited the verse, "Nay! But they are a quarrelsome people."[52] Maryam ﷺ was directed not to debate or argue with her people because they had already made up their minds and come to their own conclusion. The only thing that would convince them is the miraculous speech of ʿIsā ﷺ from the cradle.

7.

Self-Confidence - As people of faith, we are supposed to be confident in our beliefs, practices, and identity. We should not be ashamed of who we are. Our conduct and behavior in society and in public should be bold and thoughtful; it should show absolute, 100% conviction and belief in the message that Allah ﷻ has given us. Our actions, the way we behave, interact with others and conduct business should be a reflection of our faith in Allah ﷻ and His Messenger ﷺ. We should live with honor, dignity, and pride. We shouldn't feel intimidated in any way, shape, or form. We shouldn't have an inferiority complex. We should feel pride in our dīn and wear it on our sleeves.

8.

Tarbiyah (proper upbringing) - Children are considered to be a reflection of their parents and are expected to live up to their moral standards. That's why it's extremely important to impart a moral upbringing along with academic education. As a matter of fact, the most important things to focus on when raising a child are their beliefs and character.

9.

ʿUbūdiyyah - The highest rank or station we can achieve in this world is that of an ʿabd, a slave of Allah ﷻ. The purpose of our life and existence is to worship Allah ﷻ through submission, devotion, obedience, servitude, and

52 ibn Mājah, *k. al-muqaddimah*, 48

gratitude. Allah ﷻ says, "I created jinn and mankind only to worship Me."[53]

10.

Be a Source of Benefit - One of the best acts of worship we can engage in is to be of service and benefit to others. The Prophet ﷺ told us, "Whoever relieves the distress/difficulty of a believer from the difficulties of this world, then Allah will remove a difficulty from the difficulties of the Day of Judgment for him. And whoever alleviates the need of a needy person, Allah will alleviate his needs in this world and the Hereafter. Whoever conceals the faults of a Muslim, Allah will conceal his faults in this life and the next. And Allah will aid His slave so long as he aids his brother."[54] In another ḥadīth the Prophet ﷺ told us, "The most beloved servants to Allah ﷻ are those who are of the most benefit to people."[55] One of the greatest and most virtuous acts a person can engage in is serving and helping others. The Prophet ﷺ said, "Among the best of deeds is to make a believer happy; to clothe them if they are unclothed, to feed them if they are hungry, and to fulfill their needs."[56]

11.

The Importance of Ṣalāh and Zakāh - These are among the five pillars of Islam and are the two acts of worship that are most often paired together throughout the Quran and ḥadīth.

12.

Humility - Humility is one of the most important qualities or characteristics that we are supposed to nurture and develop within ourselves. It is the opposite of being proud and arrogant. The Prophet ﷺ told us, "No one humbles themselves for the sake of Allah ﷻ except that Allah ﷻ elevates them."[57]

---

53 وَمَا خَلَقْتُ الْجِنَّ وَالْإِنسَ إِلَّا لِيَعْبُدُونِ - 51:56

54 Muslim, *k. al-dhikr wa al-duʿā wa al-tawbah wa al-istighfār, b. faḍl al-ijtimāʿ ʿalā tilāwah al-quran wa ʿalā al-dhikr,* 2699

55 Abū Nuʿaim, *Hilyah al-Awliyā',* 6:348

56 al-Mundhirī, *al-Targhīb wa al-Tarhīb,* 3:346

57 Muslim, *k. al-birr wa al-ṣilah wa al-ādāb, b. istiḥbāb al-ʿafw wa al-tawāḍuʿ,* 2588

13.

Allah ﷻ Grants the Wrongdoers Respite - Allah ﷻ through His infinite grace and mercy doesn't hold the wrongdoers accountable immediately. He ﷻ grants them time to either recognize their mistakes and change their ways, or to dig a deeper hole for themselves. The phenomenon of allowing the evil and corrupt to continue down their path of misguidance unaware is known as istidrāj. A person is taken down the path of destruction in very small, incremental degrees.

In the next passage, Allah ﷻ briefly mentions an episode from the life of Ibrāhīm ﵇. Allah ﷻ narrates a conversation Ibrāhīm ﵇ had with his father when he was a child. This is the third story mentioned in the sūrah; the first was the story of Zakariyya ﵇ and the second was the story of Maryam ﵇ and the miraculous birth of ʿIsā ﵇.

This Sūrah is unique in that it's giving us glimpses into different types of relationships. The beginning of the Sūrah explored the relationship between a father and son, from the perspective of the father. The next story showed the relationship between a mother and son. Now Allah ﷻ shows us a relationship between a son and his father, from the perspective of the son.

One of the central themes of this Sūrah in addition to mercy is tawḥīd, the oneness of Allah ﷻ. This story deals with that concept in a very clear and eloquent manner. Allah ﷻ starts this passage by telling the Prophet ﷺ to mention and remind his people of the story of Ibrāhīm ﵇.

VERSE 41

وَٱذْكُرْ فِى ٱلْكِتَـٰبِ إِبْرَٰهِيمَ ۚ إِنَّهُۥ كَانَ صِدِّيقًا نَّبِيًّا

And mention in the Book [the story of] Ibrāhīm. He was surely a man of truth and a prophet.

In this verse, Allah ﷻ is addressing the Prophet ﷺ and telling him to remember the story of Ibrāhīm ﷺ - the truthful Prophet, the friend of Allah ﷻ, and the father of Prophets - himself, and to mention it to others by reciting it to them from the Quran.

Allah ﷻ then describes Ibrāhīm ﷺ with two characteristics: very truthful and a prophet. The word "ṣiddīq" is on the word pattern of ṣīghah al-mubālaghah from the root letters ṣād/ḍād/qāf, which mean truth and honesty. It gives the meaning of exaggeration and excess. Ibrāhīm ﷺ is being described as someone who is extremely honest and truthful. He always told the truth and never told a lie. His actions were always honest; meaning he was sincere in his beliefs and actions. His actions always matched his words. It could also mean that he always accepted what Allah ﷻ commanded him to do. He always accepted the commands of Allah ﷻ without any hesitation whatsoever. For example, when he was told to leave Hājar and Ismāʿīl in the middle of the desert with no wealth, water, or food he did so without any hesitation whatsoever. Similarly, when he was told to sacrifice his son Ismāʿīl ﷺ, he did so without the slightest hesitation whatsoever. That is one of the reasons why Abū Bakr ؓ was given the title al-Ṣiddīq; he accepted the call of the Prophet ﷺ without any hesitation whatsoever.

The second description is that he was a prophet. He was chosen and selected by Allah ﷻ to serve as a prophet for his community. Theologians and scholars differentiate between the word "prophet" and the word "messenger."

The most common distinction that's mentioned is that a prophet is an individual that receives revelation (waḥy) from Allah ﷻ and is told to invite his people towards belief. A messenger is also an individual that receives revelation from Allah ﷻ, but they are given a scripture or a new system of law and are told to invite their community towards it. Every messenger is a prophet, but not every prophet is a messenger. Although only the word prophet is used here to describe Ibrāhīm عليه السلام, we learn from other verses that he was a messenger as well.

Allah ﷻ then relates the conversation Ibrāhīm عليه السلام had with his father regarding belief and polytheism. His father's name was Āzar. He was an idol worshipper and used to make and sell the idols that people worshipped. There are two main reasons for mentioning this story here:

1.

Reminder to the people of Quraysh - The people of Quraysh were familiar with the story of Ibrāhīm عليه السلام and actually claimed to be following his teachings. Through the story of Ibrāhīm عليه السلام mentioned in the Quran, Allah ﷻ shows the polytheists of Makkah how far they have strayed from the true teachings of Ibrāhīm عليه السلام.

2.

Consolation for the Prophet ﷺ and his Companions رضي الله عنهم.

VERSE 42

إِذْ قَالَ لِأَبِيهِ يَـٰٓأَبَتِ لِمَ تَعْبُدُ مَا لَا يَسْمَعُ وَلَا يُبْصِرُ وَلَا يُغْنِى
عَنكَ شَيْـًٔا

[Remember] when he said to his father, "O my dear father! Why do you worship that which does not hear and does not see and will not benefit you at all?

Allah ﷻ is continuing to address the Prophet ﷺ and is telling him to remember and remind his people of the time when Ibrāhīm ﷺ said to his father Āzar, "O my dear father, why do you worship that which does not hear and does not see and will not benefit you at all?" Ibrāhīm ﷺ was sent to change and eradicate the religion and way of life of his father, yet he still addressed him with the utmost love, honor, and respect. The word "abatī" is an expression of endearment, which is best translated as "my dear father". It is an expression that conveys deep respect and love for one's father.

This is a perfect example of how we are supposed to advise people and invite them towards the truth with sincere care, concern, gentleness, and love. His father is living a life of disbelief, associating partners with Allah ﷻ, and misguidance. He's calling others to follow his way as well and is the one who sculpts and sells statues and idols that people worship. Ibrāhīm ﷺ was sent to change those beliefs and invite people towards the truth. His hatred and dislike for those beliefs didn't turn into hatred and dislike for his father. Rather, he maintains that love and respect. He doesn't use harsh, rude, and abusive language or any words that could hurt his father's pride or feelings.

First, he drew his father's attention to the helplessness of the idols. Why do you worship something that can't hear when you call upon it? Why do you worship something that can't even see what you're doing for it? Why do you worship something that can't benefit you and can't prevent harm from you? Through this verse, Allah ﷻ is teaching the Prophet ﷺ how to address his own people, the people of Quraysh. He's also being taught how to bring people's attention to the fallacies of their beliefs. You can't just tell someone they're wrong, but you have to make them realize why. These same questions that Ibrāhīm ﷺ is asking his father are being addressed to the people of Quraysh.

Next, he tells his father that he has been given unique prophetic knowledge from Allah ﷻ. He's explaining why he's bringing this topic up and what he would like his father to do.

VERSE 43

يَـٰٓأَبَتِ إِنِّى قَدْ جَآءَنِى مِنَ ٱلْعِلْمِ مَا لَمْ يَأْتِكَ فَٱتَّبِعْنِىٓ أَهْدِكَ
صِرَٰطًا سَوِيًّا

O my dear father! I have certainly received some knowledge that you have not received, so follow me and I will guide you to an even path.

Again he addresses his father with love, respect, and honor; with words of endearment to soften his heart and make it more accepting of the truth. He's softening the heart of his father because the softer the heart, the easier it is to get the person to actually listen and be convinced. He tells him that even though I'm your son and I'm younger than you, I have been given some knowledge from Allah ﷻ that you have not been given. I have been given knowledge regarding truth and reality; the existence and oneness of Allah ﷻ. By saying this he's trying to pre-empt his father's rejection of the previous statement. It is as if he's saying, "Please listen to me with an open heart and mind because I'm speaking based on knowledge and understanding. Follow me in my sincere advice and I will guide you to the straight path."

Again, Ibrāhīm ﷺ is showing us the proper way of advising and giving good counsel. We can't start by telling someone to follow us because we know more and that they are ignorant. That comes off as very arrogant and rude and will turn most people away. That's why Ibrāhīm ﷺ didn't call his father ignorant nor did he describe himself as being more knowledgeable. His words, despite his young age, are full of wisdom. He then warns his father with a sense of genuine and sincere concern.

VERSE 44

يَٰٓأَبَتِ لَا تَعۡبُدِ ٱلشَّيۡطَٰنَۖ إِنَّ ٱلشَّيۡطَٰنَ كَانَ لِلرَّحۡمَٰنِ عَصِيّٗا

O my dear father! Do not worship Satan. Indeed Satan is ever rebellious against the Most Merciful.

Once again, he starts with that expression of love and care, "yā abatī," O my dear beloved father. "Don't worship Satan." Meaning, don't follow and obey Satan by worshipping idols and associating partners with Allah ﷻ. Āzar wasn't a Satan worshipper, but he was misguided by Satan to worship idols; idol worship comes from the whispers of Satan. Ibrāhīm ﵇ is appealing to his sense of morality. Don't follow Satan and then he mentions the reason why. "Indeed Satan is ever rebellious against the Most Merciful." He's the one who has consistently been disobedient to Allah ﷻ since the creation of Adam ﵇. The word عَصِيًّا is also on the word pattern of ṣīghah al-mubālagha. He's always and consistently disobeying Allah ﷻ and trying to lead as many human beings astray as possible. Satan is not your friend; rather, he is your sworn enemy so beware of following in his footsteps. Ibrāhīm ﵇ then mentions his concern for his father.

VERSE 45

يَـٰٓأَبَتِ إِنِّىٓ أَخَافُ أَن يَمَسَّكَ عَذَابٌ مِّنَ ٱلرَّحْمَـٰنِ فَتَكُونَ لِلشَّيْطَـٰنِ وَلِيًّا

O my dear father! I truly fear that a punishment from the Lord of Mercy may afflict you and that you may become Satan's companion [in Hellfire].

This verse is full of genuine, sincere, and true concern for the safety and protection of his father. This is not a concern for his physical or financial safety; it is a concern for his spiritual safety and eternal salvation. He is telling his father that if you continue to worship idols I fear that the punishment of Allah ﷻ, the Most Merciful, will come upon you. And as a result of that punishment, you will be Satan's companion in Hell. This is a warning to his father, but not in a rude or threatening way. The language used here is also very precise and purposeful; every single word of the Quran is chosen for a reason. Here, Allah ﷻ juxtaposes His punishment with His mercy. "I truly fear that a punishment from the Lord of Mercy may afflict you." Ibrāhīm عليه السلام chose to mention Allah ﷻ with His attribute of mercy as a gentle reminder to his father that Allah ﷻ is absolutely and infinitely merciful. Despite your past sins, despite your beliefs and idol worship, if you turn to Allah ﷻ, He will shower you with His mercy and grace.

Despite the amount of humility, respect, care, concern, and love Ibrāhīm عليه السلام showed for his father, he still replied with anger in an extremely harsh manner. He responded with threats of physical punishment and asked him to leave. This was a severe and emotional test for Ibrāhīm عليه السلام.

VERSE 46

قَالَ أَرَاغِبٌ أَنتَ عَنْ ءَالِهَتِى يَٰٓإِبْرَٰهِيمُ ۖ لَئِن لَّمْ تَنتَهِ لَأَرْجُمَنَّكَ ۖ وَٱهْجُرْنِى مَلِيًّا

[His father] said, "Do you reject my gods, O Ibrāhīm? If you do not desist, I will surely stone you, so be gone from me for a long time."

In Arabic, the verb "raghiba" is used with two different particles, and they give two opposite meanings. "Raghiba fī" means to desire or want something; to like it. "Raghiba ʿan" means to be averse to something; to not like it. Āzar is asking his son in anger and astonishment, "Do you reject my gods, O Ibrāhīm?" Are you turning away from my deities? Are you rejecting them and leaving their worship? If you don't want to worship them then don't, but stop speaking against them and pointing out their weaknesses. If you don't stop speaking against them, then I will stone you. He's threatening his own son, his flesh and blood, with actual physical violence. Stop or I'll stone you. "And leave me for a long period of time!" He's telling his own son to leave and get lost. In a sense, he's disowning him.

Imagine how Ibrāhīm ﷷ must have felt at this moment; rejected, threatened, and disowned by his own flesh and bold, his own father. This is the exact same feeling that the Prophet ﷺ was going through as well. Allah ﷻ is teaching the Prophet ﷺ how to respond and react in that type of situation. Look at how Ibrāhīm ﷷ responded to his father and follow his example.

VERSE 47

قَالَ سَلَمٌ عَلَيْكَ ۖ سَأَسْتَغْفِرُ لَكَ رَبِّىٓ ۖ إِنَّهُۥ كَانَ بِى حَفِيًّا

[Ibrāhīm] said, "You are safe and secure [from harm]. I will seek forgiveness for you from my Lord. Indeed, He has always been gracious to me.

Ibrāhīm ⬡ responded to his father's harshness, anger, and threat calmly saying, "You are safe and secure [from harm]." He's ending the conversation and relationship with his father with politeness and kindness. He doesn't want to cause his father any harm whatsoever. This is exactly what Allah ⬡ directs us to do in the Quran when engaged in a conversation with someone who is hostile. "When ignorant people speak to them they say salām."[58] Instead of getting into an argument with them, just say salām and leave the conversation. Ibrāhīm ⬡ is saying good-bye to his father in a beautiful way and that he won't harm him in any way; he will be safe and secure from him. He also tells him "I will seek forgiveness for you from my Lord." This highlights that he's not angry or upset with his father; rather he tells him that he will still pray for his forgiveness and guidance. Ibrāhīm ⬡ is still concerned for the salvation of his father.

Here the scholars of tafsīr mention a common objection. Why did Ibrāhīm ⬡ say he would seek forgiveness for his father, when it is impermissible to seek forgiveness for a nonbeliever? The proof for this is that after Abū Ṭālib, the uncle of the Prophet ⬡, passed away the Prophet ⬡ said, "By Allah, I will seek forgiveness for you as long as I'm not forbidden to do so." After he said that the prohibition was revealed, "It is not [proper] for the Prophet and the believers to seek forgiveness for the polytheists, even if they

---

58   وَإِذَا خَاطَبَهُمُ الْجَاهِلُونَ قَالُوا سَلَامًا - 25:63

were close relatives, after it has become clear to the believers that they are bound for the Hellfire."[59] After the revelation of this verse, he stopped seeking forgiveness for his uncle.

The answer to this objection is that Ibrāhīm made this promise to his father before it was prohibited. Allah ﷻ explains this Himself saying, "As for Ibrāhīm's prayer for his father's forgiveness, it was only in fulfilment of a promise he had made to him. But when it became clear to Ibrāhīm that his father was an enemy of Allah, he broke ties with him. Ibrāhīm was truly tender-hearted, forbearing."[60] To be clear, we are allowed to pray for the guidance of a nonbeliever as long as they are alive. If they pass away on disbelief, then it is no longer permissible to pray for them.

"Indeed, He has always been gracious to me." Meaning, Allah ﷻ has always taken care of me and will always take care of me. He ﷻ listens to my prayers and answers them, shading me with His divine protection, security, mercy, grace, and guidance.

Ibrāhīm then informs his father of his decision to leave his people and their religion completely and to migrate somewhere else.

VERSE 48

وَأَعْتَزِلُكُمْ وَمَا تَدْعُونَ مِن دُونِ ٱللَّهِ وَأَدْعُوا رَبِّي عَسَىٰٓ أَلَّآ أَكُونَ بِدُعَآءِ رَبِّي شَقِيًّا

And I will leave you and those you invoke other than Allah

---

59   Bukhārī, k. al-tafsīr, b. qawlihi mā kāna li al-nabiyy wa alladhīna āmanu an yastaghfi-ru li al-mushrikīn, 4675

60   وَمَا كَانَ ٱسْتِغْفَارُ إِبْرَاهِيمَ لِأَبِيهِ إِلَّا عَن مَّوْعِدَةٍ وَعَدَهَا إِيَّاهُ فَلَمَّا تَبَيَّنَ لَهُ أَنَّهُ - 9:114 عَدُوٌّ لِّلَّهِ تَبَرَّأَ مِنْهُ إِنَّ إِبْرَاهِيمَ لَأَوَّاهٌ حَلِيمٌ

and will invoke my Lord, trusting that I will never be disappointed in invoking my Lord.

Ibrāhīm ﷺ is telling his father that he will withdraw and leave him, move away with his religion, and abandon and dissociate himself from what he worships besides Allah ﷻ. He declares that he will worship Allah ﷻ alone without any partners, submitting himself completely to His devotion and worship. The word "ʿasā" means perhaps, and it gives the meaning of being hopeful or having expectations. Ibrāhīm ﷺ is hopeful and trusts that Allah ﷻ will answer his prayers. He says this out of humility, because in reality he has absolute conviction that Allah ﷻ will answer his prayers. One of the reasons for mentioning this is to show the contrast between his relationship with Allah ﷻ and the polytheists' relationship with their idols. Allah ﷻ answers those who call upon Him helping and assisting them; whereas, the idols are inanimate objects that do not respond when they are called upon. They can't even hear supplications, so how would they respond? When he left his people and migrated for the sake of his faith and the truth, Allah ﷻ fulfilled his hope and answered his prayer.

VERSE 49

فَلَمَّا ٱعْتَزَلَهُمْ وَمَا يَعْبُدُونَ مِن دُونِ ٱللَّهِ وَهَبْنَا لَهُۥٓ إِسْحَٰقَ
وَيَعْقُوبَ ۖ وَكُلًّا جَعَلْنَا نَبِيًّا

So after he had left them and what they worshipped besides Allah, We granted him Isḥāq and Yaʿqūb, and made each of them a prophet.

When Ibrāhīm ﵇ withdrew from his father and his people, when he left his home and family, migrating for the truth and his beliefs, Allah ﷻ fulfilled his hope. He ﷻ did so by giving him the gift of a son, Isḥāq ﵇, and a grandson, Yaʿqūb ﵇. Isḥāq ﵇ is the son of Sārah. The Quran doesn't mention much from his story except that the angels gave Ibrāhīm ﵇ glad tidings regarding him. Yaʿqūb ﵇, Isḥāq's son, was the father of Yūsuf ﵇. Allah ﷻ, through His infinite grace and mercy, replaced his father and people with a family that was much better than them. Both of them were also selected and chosen as prophets.

VERSE 50

وَوَهَبْنَا لَهُم مِّن رَّحْمَتِنَا وَجَعَلْنَا لَهُمْ لِسَانَ صِدْقٍ عَلِيًّا

We showered them with Our mercy, and blessed them with honourable mention.

Allah ﷻ showered all of them - Ibrāhīm, Isḥāq, and Yaʿqūb - with His infinite and limitless grace and mercy. Allah ﷻ selected each of them as prophets and blessed them with wealth, children, and scripture. He ﷻ also blessed them "with honourable mention." Part of what that means is that they are held in high respect and honor in all religions. Every Abrahamic religion - the Jews, Christians, and we as Muslims, hold them in the highest regard and praise them.

LESSONS AND BENEFITS FROM THE STORY OF IBRĀHĪM (عليه السلام)

1.

Inviting Towards Allah ﷻ with Beauty and Wisdom - One of the most important lessons we learn in this episode from the life of Ibrāhīm (عليه السلام) is the methodology of inviting others towards the truth. When inviting others towards Allah ﷻ, it is extremely important to remember the proper etiquette and manners of doing so. A person should try their best to be wise, gentle, caring, sincere, compassionate, forbearing, forgiving, and patient. They should not be the cause of driving people further away from Allah ﷻ and religion. Rather, they should be the means of bringing people closer to Allah ﷻ. That is one of the reasons why the Prophet ﷺ taught his Companions, "Give glad tidings and don't push people away. Make things easy and don't make things difficult."[61] They should not be harsh, abrasive, rude, and impatient, thus becoming a means for people to be pushed away.

Allah ﷻ says in Sūrah al-Naḥl, "[Prophet], call [people] to the way of your Lord with wisdom and good teaching. Argue with them in the most courteous way, for your Lord knows best who has strayed from His way and who is rightly guided."[62] In this verse, Allah ﷻ reminds the Prophet ﷺ about three very important components of inviting and reminding others; wisdom, good teaching, and courtesy. This includes being sincere, having genuine concern, gentleness, compassion, and leniency. However, there are circumstances and situations that require one to be a little more stern and sometimes even harsh. This has been the methodology of all prophets and messengers throughout history, as can be seen through their narratives that are mentioned in the Quran.

2.

Addressing Fathers with Respect - Fathers play a very important and fundamental role in the lives of their children. Within the Islamic framework,

---

61 Muslim, *k. al-jihād wa al-siyar, b. fī al-amr bi al-taysīr wa tark al-tanfīr*, 1732

62 16:125 - ادْعُ إِلَىٰ سَبِيلِ رَبِّكَ بِالْحِكْمَةِ وَالْمَوْعِظَةِ الْحَسَنَةِ ۖ وَجَادِلْهُم بِالَّتِي هِيَ أَحْسَنُ ۚ إِنَّ رَبَّكَ هُوَ أَعْلَمُ بِمَن ضَلَّ عَن سَبِيلِهِ ۖ وَهُوَ أَعْلَمُ بِالْمُهْتَدِينَ

a man is responsible and expected to exert his best effort in providing and taking care of the affairs of his family, particularly his children. The Prophet ﷺ told us, "All of you are shepherds and each of you is responsible for their flock. The ruler is a shepherd. A man is a shepherd of those under his care. A woman is a shepherd of her husband's home and children. Each of you is a shepherd and each of you is responsible for their flock."[63] A father should always be addressed with words of endearment and respect. That is part of following the command of being dutiful to one's parents.

3.

Avoid Conflict - It is always better to avoid conflict and approach conversations with wisdom and tact. Approaching contentious conversations with humility, gentleness, calm, and deliberation is a sign of intelligence, insight, and sound understanding.

4.

Absurdity of Associating Partners with Allah ﷻ - Allah ﷻ highlights in several passages throughout the Quran how absurd it is to associate partners with Him. As a matter of fact, one of the major, and perhaps the primary, themes of the Quran is to establish and explain the concept of tawḥīd, the Divine Oneness of Allah ﷻ.

5.

Genuine Concern - Our concern for our families and humanity in general is rooted in several different factors; physical, financial, emotional, and psychological. The most important concern we should have is for people's spiritual state; their relationship with Allah ﷻ. We should be concerned about their salvation in the life of the Hereafter, which was the concern of every single prophet and messenger throughout history.

6.

Importance of Knowledge - It is extremely important for our message and invitation to be based upon knowledge and understanding. In order for our message to be heard and understood properly, we ourselves have to have

63 Bukhārī, *k. al-nikāḥ, b. al-mar'ah rāʿiyah ʿalā bayt zawjihā*, 5200

a proper understanding of it. We can't have the blind leading the blind.

7.

Satan is our Open Enemy - The enmity of Satan is not something secret or hidden; it is as plain as daylight. The enmity of Satan is highlighted in several places throughout the Quran. For example, Allah ﷻ tells us, "Satan is your enemy - so treat him as an enemy - and invites his followers to enter the blazing fire." [64]

8.

Allah's ﷻ Mercy - Allah's mercy is infinite and limitless. He forgives all sins as long as we seek forgiveness from Him ﷻ and turn back to Him ﷻ in sincere repentance. Allah ﷻ expresses His divine mercy to us in a number of unique and different ways. Here we see how Allah ﷻ showered His divine mercy upon Ibrāhīm ؑ by guiding him towards the truth and blessing him with a righteous and pious family.

9.

How to Respond to Threats - Oftentimes people respond with physical and verbal threats when they are flustered and run out of options. When someone is unable to engage with your arguments intellectually, they become emotional and will resort to anger, mockery, ridicule, insults, cursing, and perhaps threats of physical violence. In situations like that, it is much better for us not to respond and engage. As mentioned above, Allah ﷻ tells us, "When ignorant people speak to them they say salām."[65]

10.

The Power and Significance of Duʿā - Allah ﷻ hears our supplications and responds. When calling upon Allah ﷻ, we should have certainty that He ﷻ will respond to our prayers according to His ﷻ divine wisdom.

---

64 إِنَّ الشَّيْطَانَ لَكُمْ عَدُوٌّ فَاتَّخِذُوهُ عَدُوًّا ۚ إِنَّمَا يَدْعُو حِزْبَهُ لِيَكُونُوا مِنْ أَصْحَابِ السَّعِيرِ - 35:6

65 وَإِذَا خَاطَبَهُمُ الْجَاهِلُونَ قَالُوا سَلَامًا - 25:63

11.

Sacrifice - Sometimes we are going to have to make sacrifices for the sake of our faith and beliefs. That sacrifice can take several different shapes and forms and be of varying degrees. However, whatever we sacrifice, Allah ﷾ will replace it with something better, either in this world, and definitely in the next.

In the next set of verses, Allah ﷻ briefly mentions a number of different prophets: Mūsa, Ismāʿīl, and Idrīs ﷺ. The main purpose of mentioning the names of these prophets and some of their attributes is to comfort and console the Prophet ﷺ. Allah ﷻ is reminding him that he is not alone in the struggles and difficulties he is facing calling his people to Islam. These are the exact same struggles and difficulties the prophets before him faced. Through these verses, Allah ﷻ is encouraging the Prophet ﷺ to remain patient and steadfast and to follow the example of the prophets before him. Through these brief references, Allah ﷻ is strengthening his resolve and determination. Allah ﷻ tells him,

VERSE 51

وَٱذْكُرْ فِى ٱلْكِتَـٰبِ مُوسَىٰٓ ۚ إِنَّهُۥ كَانَ مُخْلَصًا وَكَانَ رَسُولًا نَّبِيًّا

And mention in the Book [the story of] Mūsa. Indeed he

was chosen, and he was a messenger and a prophet.

Allah ﷻ is speaking directly to the Prophet ﷺ and telling him to remember the story of Mūsa ﷇ mentioned in the Quran and to mention the story to his community. This is the fifth story mentioned in the Sūrah after the stories of Zakariyyā, Yaḥyā, Maryam, and Ibrāhīm ﷈. Here, Allah ﷻ is only making a brief reference to the story of Mūsa ﷇ that has been mentioned in detail throughout other parts of the Quran, highlighting some unique qualities and characteristics of this noble Prophet and Messenger.

Allah ﷻ starts by saying, "Indeed he was chosen." This word "mukhlaṣ" can be recited in two different ways, with a fatḥah on the "lām" or with a kasrah on the "lām," which conveys different shades of meaning.

If it is recited with a fatḥah on the "lām" - mukhlaṣ - it gives the meaning of being chosen, being purified, and protected. It is the passive participle from the verb akhlaṣa/yukhliṣu, which means to dedicate, be devoted, loyal, or faithful. It means that Mūsa ﷇ was chosen by Allah ﷻ to receive revelation and be a prophet and messenger. As Allah ﷻ says in Sūrah al-Aʿrāf, "[Allah] said, 'O Mūsa, I have chosen you over the people with My messages and My words [to you]. So take what I have given you and be among the grateful.'"[66] It could also mean that he has been protected from sins and disobedience.

If it is recited with a kasrah on the "lām" - mukhliṣ - it gives the meaning of being sincere. Meaning, Mūsa ﷇ was sincere in his worship and obedience to Allah ﷻ. Sincerity is a central characteristic of our relationship with Allah ﷻ. It is described as doing something solely for the sake of Allah ﷻ, without the desire of recognition, fame, or anything else.

"And he was a messenger and a prophet." Mūsa ﷇ was both a messenger and a prophet, just like our beloved Muḥammad ﷺ, the Seal of all prophets and messengers. As mentioned earlier, scholars differentiate between the word "prophet" and the word "messenger." The most common distinction that's mentioned is that a prophet is an individual that receives revelation (waḥy) from Allah ﷻ and is told to invite his people towards belief. A messenger is also an individual that receives revelation from Allah ﷻ, but is

66 7:144 - قَالَ يَا مُوسَىٰ إِنِّي اصْطَفَيْتُكَ عَلَى النَّاسِ بِرِسَالَاتِي وَبِكَلَامِي فَخُذْ مَا آتَيْتُكَ وَكُن مِّنَ الشَّاكِرِينَ

given a scripture or a new system of law and is told to invite his community towards it. Every messenger is a prophet, but not every prophet is a messenger. Mūsa ؑ was both and is considered to be among the prophets that are described as the Messengers of Firm Resolve (Ulu al-ʿAzm min al-Rusul).

VERSE 52

وَنَٰدَيْنَٰهُ مِن جَانِبِ ٱلطُّورِ ٱلْأَيْمَنِ وَقَرَّبْنَٰهُ نَجِيًّا

And We called him from the right side of Mount Ṭūr, and drew him near, speaking [with him] directly.

In this verse, Allah ﷻ is briefly referring to a part of the story of Mūsa ؑ, specifically the time when he was appointed as a prophet and messenger. "And We called him" means that Allah ﷻ called out to him and spoke to him directly. That's why Mūsa ؑ has been given the nickname Kalīmullah, the one who spoke directly to Allah ﷻ. This is where and when Allah ﷻ appointed him as a prophet and messenger for the Children of Israel. "From the right side of Mount Ṭūr" is referring to the fact that Allah ﷻ spoke to him from the side of the mountain that was to the right of Mūsa ؑ. This incident took place when Mūsa ؑ was on his way back to Egypt from Madyan. "And drew him near, speaking [with him] directly." This isn't referring to physical nearness, but a spiritual nearness; nearness and proximity in terms of relationship, honor, rank, and status.

VERSE 53

وَوَهَبْنَا لَهُۥ مِن رَّحْمَتِنَآ أَخَاهُ هَـٰرُونَ نَبِيًّا

And We granted him out of Our mercy his brother Hārūn as a prophet.

The verb wahaba/yahibu, to give or gift, in the Quran is usually associated with children; the gift of offspring, as we saw earlier with Zakariyyā عليه السلام. Here Allah سبحانه وتعالى is telling Mūsa عليه السلام that He has chosen his brother Hārūn عليه السلام to be a prophet along with him. And this gift, like all others, is from the infinite mercy and grace of Allah سبحانه وتعالى. Mūsa عليه السلام asked Allah سبحانه وتعالى to make his older brother Hārūn a prophet along with him. Allah سبحانه وتعالى tells us in Sūrah ṬāHā that Mūsa عليه السلام said, "And appoint for me a minister from my family - Hārūn, my brother. Increase through him my strength. And let him share my task. That we may exalt You much. And remember You much. Indeed, You are of us ever-Seeing." [Allah] said, "You have been granted your request, O Mūsa."[67] That's why Hārūn عليه السلام is known as Hibah Allah, the gift of Allah. Allah سبحانه وتعالى then mentions Ismāʿīl عليه السلام and some of his characteristics.

---

67 20:29-36 - وَٱجْعَل لِّى وَزِيرًا مِّنْ أَهْلِى * هَـٰرُونَ أَخِى * ٱشْدُدْ بِهِۦٓ أَزْرِى ﴿٣١﴾ وَأَشْرِكْهُ فِىٓ أَمْرِى * كَىْ نُسَبِّحَكَ كَثِيرًا * وَنَذْكُرَكَ كَثِيرًا * إِنَّكَ كُنتَ بِنَا بَصِيرًا * قَالَ قَدْ أُوتِيتَ سُؤْلَكَ يَـٰمُوسَىٰ

VERSE 54

وَٱذْكُرْ فِى ٱلْكِتَٰبِ إِسْمَٰعِيلَ ۚ إِنَّهُۥ كَانَ صَادِقَ ٱلْوَعْدِ وَكَانَ رَسُولًا
نَّبِيًّا

And mention in the Book, Ismāʿīl. Indeed, he was true to his promise, and he was a messenger and a prophet.

Again Allah ﷻ is directly addressing the Prophet ﷺ and telling him to remember Ismāʿīl عليه السلام and to mention his story as it's related in the Quran. This is the sixth story mentioned in this Sūrah, the story of Ismāʿīl عليه السلام the son of Ibrāhīm عليه السلام, who he was commanded to sacrifice through his dream. Allah ﷻ describes Ismāʿīl عليه السلام with four attributes.

The first is that he was a man of his word. "Indeed he was true to his promise." He is being described with the universal qualities and values of honesty and integrity. These are two morals that are universal; every single religion or way of life encourages them and looks down upon dishonesty. He was someone who always fulfilled his promises, whether those promises were to Allah ﷻ or to people. He always kept his word and never went against anything he was commanded to do. He fulfilled his promise to his father that he would be patient with the command of Allah ﷻ to sacrifice him, which is the epitome of submission and loyalty. When Ibrāhīm عليه السلام told him about the dream, he responded without any hesitation whatsoever saying, "O my dear father! Do as you are commanded. Allah willing, you will find me steadfast."[68]

As an anecdote of his truthfulness and honesty, it's mentioned that once he promised to meet someone at a specific place and time. That person didn't

68 قَالَ يَا أَبَتِ افْعَلْ مَا تُؤْمَرُ ۖ سَتَجِدُنِي إِن شَاءَ اللَّهُ مِنَ الصَّابِرِينَ - 37:102

show up and he waited there for three days.[69]

Honesty and integrity are qualities of the righteous that we are encouraged to nurture and develop within ourselves. Allah ﷻ says in Sūrah al-Ṣaff, "O you who have believed, why do you say what you do not do? Great is hatred in the sight of Allah that you say what you do not do."[70] Similarly, the Prophet ﷺ said, "The signs of a hypocrite a three; when he speaks he lies, when he makes a promise he breaks it, and when he is entrusted he breaks the trust."[71] The Prophet ﷺ also said, "The promise is a debt." [72]

Allah ﷻ then tells us that he was also "a messenger and a prophet." Ismāʿīl ؑ was both a messenger and a prophet just like his father. He was a messenger sent to the people of Jurhum in Makkah, inviting them towards the code of law and way of life that was revealed to his father Ibrāhīm ؑ.

VERSE 55

وَكَانَ يَأْمُرُ أَهْلَهُۥ بِٱلصَّلَوٰةِ وَٱلزَّكَوٰةِ وَكَانَ عِندَ رَبِّهِۦ مَرْضِيًّا

And he used to command his people with prayer and zakāh and his Lord was well pleased with him.

Ismāʿīl ؑ used to teach his people, community, and family about these two very important and fundamental acts of worship; prayer and zakāh. These are the two most important acts of worship and devotion that

69 Qurṭubī, *al-Jāmiʿ fī Aḥkām al-Quran*, 13:463

70 61:2-3 - يَا أَيُّهَا الَّذِينَ آمَنُوا لِمَ تَقُولُونَ مَا لَا تَفْعَلُونَ * كَبُرَ مَقْتًا عِندَ اللَّهِ أَن تَقُولُوا مَا لَا تَفْعَلُونَ

71 Bukhārī, *k. al-adab, b. qawl Allah taʿāla [yā ayyuha alladhina āman ittaqū Allah wa kūnu maʿ al-ṣādiqīn] wa mā yunha ʿan al-kadhib*, 6095

72 Ṭabarānī, *al-Muʿjam al-Awsaṭ*, 3514

have been established and practiced by all prophets and messengers. Prayer and zakāh were legislated in each of their traditions although the finer details may have differed.

Here Allah ﷻ is showing us how important it is for us to lead by example and to give good tarbiyyah to our families. It's an obligation upon us to look after the religious and spiritual development of our families. It's our responsibility to look after their religious training and knowledge. Allah ﷻ tells us in Sūrah al-Taḥrīm, "O believers! Protect yourselves and your families from a Fire whose fuel is people and stones, overseen by formidable and severe angels, who never disobey whatever Allah orders—always doing as commanded."[73] The Prophet ﷺ was told, "Order your people to pray, and pray steadfastly yourself. We are not asking you to give Us provision; We provide for you, and the rewards of the Hereafter belong to the devout." [74]

There's a beautiful ḥadīth from the Prophet ﷺ in which he tells us, "May Allah ﷻ have mercy on a man who wakes up in the night to pray and wakes up his wife. If she refuses to wake up he sprinkles water on her face. May Allah ﷻ have mercy on a woman who wakes up in the night to pray and wakes her husband up. If he refuses to wake up she sprinkles water on his face."[75] There's another similar narration that states, "If a man wakes up in the night and he wakes up his wife and they pray two units, then they will be written amongst those who remember Allah abundantly."[76]

Allah ﷻ concludes the description of Ismāʿīl عليه السلام saying, "And his Lord was well pleased with him." He was someone who through his words, actions, behavior, and character earned the pleasure and approval of Allah ﷻ. He was someone who was accepted by Allah ﷻ. The concept of acceptance is extremely important in terms of our relationship with Allah ﷻ. This is direct guidance for us to follow in his footsteps and in the footsteps of all the prophets and messengers.

Allah ﷻ now briefly mentions the story of Idrīs عليه السلام.

---

73 66:6 - يَا أَيُّهَا الَّذِينَ آمَنُوا قُوا أَنفُسَكُمْ وَأَهْلِيكُمْ نَارًا وَقُودُهَا النَّاسُ وَالْحِجَارَةُ عَلَيْهَا مَلَائِكَةٌ غِلَاظٌ شِدَادٌ لَّا يَعْصُونَ اللَّهَ مَا أَمَرَهُمْ وَيَفْعَلُونَ مَا يُؤْمَرُونَ

74 20:132 - وَأْمُرْ أَهْلَكَ بِالصَّلَاةِ وَاصْطَبِرْ عَلَيْهَا ۖ لَا نَسْأَلُكَ رِزْقًا ۖ نَّحْنُ نَرْزُقُكَ ۗ وَالْعَاقِبَةُ لِلتَّقْوَىٰ

75 Abū Dāwūd, *k. al-taṭawwuʿ*, *b. Qiyām al-layl*, 1308

76 ibn Mājah, *k. iqāmah al-ṣalah wa al-sunnah fīha*, 1396

VERSE 56

وَٱذْكُرْ فِى ٱلْكِتَـٰبِ إِدْرِيسَ ۚ إِنَّهُۥ كَانَ صِدِّيقًا نَّبِيًّا

And mention in the Book Idrīs. Indeed, he was a man of truth, and a prophet.

This is now the seventh story that is being referenced in this Sūrah, and like all the others it is mentioned for deriving lessons and morals. Idrīs is the paternal grandfather of Nūḥ ﷺ. It's narrated that his name is derived from the word "dars," which means a lesson. Some narrations mention that he received thirty revelations. He was the first man to write with a pen, stitch clothes, and learn the sciences of astrology and math, and the first to measure and use weapons.[77] He was the first prophet sent after Adam ﷺ and lived 1,000 years before Nūḥ ﷺ. The Prophet ﷺ passed by him in the fourth sky on his ascension through the heavens. He called toward the oneness of Allah ﷻ, worship of Him ﷻ alone without any partners, righteous deeds, and justice. He invited his people towards submission to Allah ﷻ through devotion, worship, servitude, and universal values. Some tafāsīr mention that he used to have a ring with the inscription, "Patience with faith in Allah leads to victory." Another saying from him is, "The fortunate one is he who looks at himself, and his intercession for him with his Lord is his righteous deeds."[78]

Allah ﷻ describes him with three attributes. The first is "Indeed he was a man of truth." The meaning of "ṣiddīq" was covered earlier when Allah ﷻ was describing Ibrāhīm ﷺ, as it's the same word that was used to describe him. He was always honest and truthful and he readily and eagerly accepted

77 Qurṭubī, *al-Jāmiʿ fī Aḥkām al-Quran*, 13:466

78 Zuḥaylī, *al-Tafsīr al-Munīr*, 8:465

the commands of Allah ﷻ. The second description is that he was "a prophet." He was sent to his people to invite them towards the truth, towards belief in Allah ﷻ, life after death, reward and punishment, paradise and Hell, righteous deeds, morals, values, and principles.

VERSE 57

وَرَفَعْنَـٰهُ مَكَانًا عَلِيًّا

And We elevated him to a high position.

This is the third description of Idrīs ﷺ. Allah ﷻ is telling us that He ﷻ granted Idrīs ﷺ a special and honorable rank and status among the prophets; he was chosen and favored by Allah ﷻ. He was granted this special rank and status because of his abundant worship. Other commentators mention that it's referring to him being physically raised to the heavens. However, this is based off of narrations from the Jews and Christians. Since the Quran isn't specific regarding what it's referring to, it's safer to go with the first explanation.

After mentioning and describing all of these prophets and messengers separately, Allah ﷻ now concludes the passage by praising all of them together. Allah ﷻ highlights that they have been blessed with prophethood and guidance, and have been chosen.

VERSE 58

أُو۟لَـٰٓئِكَ ٱلَّذِينَ أَنْعَمَ ٱللَّهُ عَلَيْهِم مِّنَ ٱلنَّبِيِّـۧنَ مِن ذُرِّيَّةِ ءَادَمَ وَمِمَّنْ
حَمَلْنَا مَعَ نُوحٍ وَمِن ذُرِّيَّةِ إِبْرَٰهِيمَ وَإِسْرَٰٓءِيلَ وَمِمَّنْ هَدَيْنَا
وَٱجْتَبَيْنَآ ۚ إِذَا تُتْلَىٰ عَلَيْهِمْ ءَايَـٰتُ ٱلرَّحْمَـٰنِ خَرُّوا۟ سُجَّدًا وَبُكِيًّا ۩

Those are [some of] the prophets who Allah has blessed from among the descendants of Adam, and of those We carried with Nūḥ [in the Ark], and of the descendants of Ibrāhīm and Isrā'īl, and of those We guided and chose. Whenever the revelations of the Most Compassionate were recited to them, they fell down, bowing and weeping.

Meaning, Allah ﷻ has chosen, selected, blessed, favored, elevated, honored, and chosen all of the prophets who have been mentioned since the beginning of the Sūrah - Zakariyyā, Yaḥyā, ʿĪsā, Ibrāhīm, Mūsa, Ismāʿīl, Idrīs - and all the other prophets and messengers throughout history. He ﷻ favored and blessed them with prophethood, messengership, guidance, and made them the best examples for humanity to follow in worship, obedience, devotion, and servitude. "Among the descendents of Adam" is a general reference referring to all prophets and messengers since all of humanity are from the descendents of Adam, or its referring to Idrīs ﷺ specifically. "And those We carried with Nūḥ [in the Ark]" refers to those prophets and messengers that were descendents of Nūḥ ﷺ, the second father of mankind. "The Descendents of Ibrāhīm and Isrā'īl ﷺ refers to Ibrāhīm's sons Ismāʿīl and Isḥāq ﷺ and the descendents of Yaʿqūb ﷺ, which include Mūsa, Hārūn, Zakariyyā, Yaḥyā, Maryam, and ʿĪsā ﷺ.

Allah ﷻ then describes all of them saying, "Whenever the revelations of the Most Compassionate were recited to them, they fell down, bowing and weeping." The revelations of Allah ﷻ that included proofs and evidences of His existence, oneness, and magnificence, His guidance and divine words, would have a direct impact upon their hearts. It would cause them to put their heads on the ground out of humility, submission, praise, and gratitude. It would pull on their emotional strings and cause them to shed tears out of their awe, reverence, honor, respect, and fear of Allah ﷻ.

LESSONS AND BENEFITS FROM THE STORIES OF PROPHETS AND MESSENGERS

1.

Sincerity - Sincerity means to worship Allah ﷻ with the sole objective or goal of attaining His nearness. Whenever a person performs an act of worship or a good deed, the intention behind it is pure; it is being done solely to seek the pleasure of Allah ﷻ. They are not looking for any type of material benefit, praise, fame, and recognition from people. Rather it is being done out of submission and obedience to Allah ﷻ; out of love for Him and to earn His mercy and forgiveness. When a person is sincere they have purified their intention and cleansed it from anything else besides Allah ﷻ. This is a quality that was possessed by all.

2.

Being Chosen by Allah ﷻ - Guidance is the realm of the Almighty; He guides whom He wills to the truth. There is no greater blessing than being guided towards faith and righteousness; it is priceless. This blessing is a unique gift from Allah ﷻ; He gives it to whom He wills and withholds it from whom He wills. However, we as human beings can do certain things that open up the path of guidance for us. Whoever turns to Allah ﷻ with an open heart and an open mind, sincerely searching for the truth, Allah ﷻ will guide them towards it.

3.

Honesty and Integrity - These are two very important values that we are supposed to nurture and develop within ourselves. They are considered to be an essential part of our īmān and identity as Muslims. A believer is a person who is honest when they speak and tries their best to keep their word. When Allah ﷻ describes true righteousness in Sūrah al-Baqarah, one of qualities mentioned is honesty. Allah ﷻ says, “Righteousness is not in turning your faces towards the east or the west. Rather, the righteous are those who believe in Allah, the Last Day, the angels, the Books, and the prophets; who give charity out of their cherished wealth to relatives, orphans, the poor, [needy] travellers, beggars, and for freeing captives; who establish ritual prayer, pay zakāh, and keep the pledges they make; and who are patient in times of suffering, adversity, and in [the heat of] battle. It is they who are true [in faith], and it is they who are mindful [of Allah].”[79]

4.

Importance of Prayer and Zakāh - Prayer and Zakāh are among the pillars of Islam and are the two acts of worship that are most commonly paired together.

5.

Tarbiyah - It is our responsibility to instill the love of Allah ﷻ, His Messenger ﷺ, and worship within the hearts and minds of our families, our wives and children, and anyone else under our care.

6.

Earning the Approval of Allah ﷻ - Earning the approval of Allah ﷻ is the ultimate goal behind everything we engage in.

7.

Responding to Revelation - Revelation should have a direct, visible, real,

79 لَّيْسَ الْبِرَّ أَن تُوَلُّوا وُجُوهَكُمْ قِبَلَ الْمَشْرِقِ وَالْمَغْرِبِ وَلَٰكِنَّ الْبِرَّ مَنْ آمَنَ بِاللَّهِ - 2:177
وَالْيَوْمِ الْآخِرِ وَالْمَلَائِكَةِ وَالْكِتَابِ وَالنَّبِيِّينَ وَآتَى الْمَالَ عَلَىٰ حُبِّهِ ذَوِي الْقُرْبَىٰ وَالْيَتَامَىٰ وَالْمَسَاكِينَ وَابْنَ
السَّبِيلِ وَالسَّائِلِينَ وَفِي الرِّقَابِ وَأَقَامَ الصَّلَاةَ وَآتَى الزَّكَاةَ وَالْمُوفُونَ بِعَهْدِهِمْ إِذَا عَاهَدُوا وَالصَّابِرِينَ فِي
الْبَأْسَاءِ وَالضَّرَّاءِ وَحِينَ الْبَأْسِ أُولَٰئِكَ الَّذِينَ صَدَقُوا وَأُولَٰئِكَ هُمُ الْمُتَّقُونَ

and transformative impact upon us. The words of Allah ﷻ should move our hearts, activate our thoughts, and inspire us towards action. We have to develop a real and intimate relationship with the words of Allah ﷻ that will help us engage with them intellectually, emotionally, and spiritually.

In the last passage, Allah ﷻ briefly referenced the stories of a number of prophets - Mūsa, Ismāʿīl, and Idrīs - as a reminder and consolation to the Prophet ﷺ and the believers. It described them and their followers with praiseworthy qualities and characteristics such as honesty, integrity, and adherence to true faith. They were the best examples of individuals who obeyed the commands of Allah ﷻ and stayed away from His prohibitions. They are described as those who have been blessed and guided by Allah ﷻ.

In the next passage, Allah ﷻ describes generations and communities who came after them and did the exact opposite. They are those who didn't fulfill their religious obligations and followed their wants and desires. Allah ﷻ mentions what their punishment will be, but makes an exception for those who repent from their mistakes and turn back to Allah ﷻ.

VERSE 59

۞ فَخَلَفَ مِنۢ بَعۡدِهِمۡ خَلۡفٌ أَضَاعُواْ ٱلصَّلَوٰةَ وَٱتَّبَعُواْ ٱلشَّهَوَٰتِ

فَسَوْفَ يَلْقَوْنَ غَيًّا ۖ

But there came after them successors who neglected prayer and pursued desires; so they are going to meet evil –

Here, Allah ﷻ is describing generations of people that came after the time of their Prophets and Messengers and slowly drifted away from their teachings. The word "khalf," with a sukūn on the lām, carries a negative connotation; it refers to bad successors. The word "khalaf," with a fatḥah on the lām, has a positive connotation; it refers to good successors. Here Allah ﷻ is speaking about bad successors; generations of people who came after their Prophets and Messengers but didn't follow their ways and teachings. It's referring to any generation of people who are misguided in their beliefs and astray in their actions. They came after those who used to truly believe in Allah ﷻ and tried their best to follow the guidance of their Prophets. These successive generations claimed to have faith and claimed to follow the teachings of their Prophets, but in reality they "neglected prayer and pursued desires."

Allah ﷻ is describing them with two negative qualities. The first is that they "neglected prayer." The commentators mention a number of different ways in which prayers are neglected.

1.

It could be referring to abandoning and leaving prayer completely; not praying at all and totally neglecting the obligation. Prayer is the most important obligation after īmān, and that is why abandoning it is something that is serious and is considered to be a major sin. It shows that a person truly doesn't care about their faith and relationship with Allah ﷻ. There are classical jursits who are of the opinion that a person who leaves prayer intentionally has left the fold of Islam. They base this position off the ḥadīth of the Prophet ﷺ, "Truly between a man and polytheism and disbelief is abandoning prayer."[80] In another narration the Prophet ﷺ said, "The agreement between me and them is prayer. Whoever leaves it has left Islam."[81] Accord-

80 Muslim, *k. al-īmān, b. bayān iṭlāq ism al-kufr ʿalā man taraka al-ṣalāh*, 82

81 Tirmidhī, *k. al-īmān ʿan rasūlillah, b. mā jā'a fī tark al-ṣalāh*, 2621

ing to the majority of scholars, abandoning prayer out of laziness or a lack of care does not take one out of the fold of Islam, but it is definitely considered to be a major sin.

2.

Neglecting prayer could be referring to delaying the obligatory prayer past its appropriate time intentionally or out of a lack of concern. Every prayer has a specific period of time in which it must be performed. Allah ﷻ says, "Indeed, performing prayers is a duty on the believers at the appointed times."[82] The Prophet ﷺ told us that one of the most virtuous deeds we can do is praying on time. The Prophet ﷺ was asked, "Which deed is the best?" He ﷺ said, "Prayer at its proper time."[83] Intentionally delaying it past its time is considered to be sinful. The Prophet ﷺ himself would always make sure to pray on time.

3.

One aspect of neglecting prayer is praying without sincerity, mindfulness, and concentration. When we pray, we should try our best to establish prayer through sincerity, mindfulness, concentration, humility, and excellence. We should try our best to pray the way the Prophet ﷺ prayed. As the Prophet ﷺ said, "Pray as you have seen me praying."[84] Rushing through prayer and being distracted are considered to be deficiencies in prayer. Once Hudhayfah رضي الله عنه saw someone praying extremely fast, so he asked him how long he had been praying like that for. The man replied for the last forty years. Hudhayfah رضي الله عنه told him, "You haven't offered a single prayer correctly."[85]

4.

According to some commentators, neglecting prayer can also refer to offering prayer at home and not in congregation in the masjid. There are several narrations from the Prophet ﷺ that highlight the importance, sig-

---

82 4:103 - إِنَّ الصَّلَاةَ كَانَتْ عَلَى الْمُؤْمِنِينَ كِتَابًا مَّوْقُوتًا

83 Muslim, *k. al-īmān, b. bayān kawn al-īmān bī Allah afḍal al-aʿmāl*, 85

84 Bukhārī, *k. al-adab, b. raḥmah al-nās wa al-bahā'im*, 6008

85 Nasā'ī, *k. al-sahw, b. tatfīf al-ṣalāh*, 1312

nificance, virtues, rewards, and blessing for praying in congregation at the masjid.

Prayer is the absolute most important act of worship we are obligated to perform. ʿUmar ﷺ sent a letter to all his governors saying, "In my view the most important amongst your tasks is prayer. Whoever neglects it, will neglect his other obligations as well."[86] The Prophet ﷺ told us, "Truly the first deed a person will be held accountable for on the Day of Judgment is their ṣalāh. If it is complete, they are successful and saved; however, if it is defective, they have failed and lost. If something is deficient in their obligatory (prayers) then the Lord, Mighty and Sublime, says, 'Look! Are there any voluntary (prayers) for my worshipper?' So with them, what was deficient in their obligatory (prayers) will be completed. Then the rest of their deeds will be dealt with in a similar manner."[87]

The second quality they are described with is that they "pursued desires." Not only did they pursue their desires but they followed them as well. "Desires" refers to everything that makes us negligent of our responsibilities to Allah ﷻ and takes us away from our true purpose in life. There are several distractions that are constantly pulling us away from the remembrance of Allah ﷻ. Allah ﷻ tells us in Sūrah Āl ʿImrān, "The enjoyment of [worldly] desires—women, children, treasures of gold and silver, fine horses, cattle, and fertile land—has been made appealing to people. These are the pleasures of this worldly life, but with Allah is the finest destination."[88] These people, the "khalf," chose their wants and desires over controlling them for the sake of Allah ﷻ. They got involved in all types of sin; zinā, drinking intoxicating beverages, false oaths, gambling, and all types of vice and immoral behavior. They became content with the life of this world and forgot about the life to come. They sacrificed eternal happiness and pleasure in the Hereafter for brief and temporary enjoyment here in the life of this world. The Prophet ﷺ said, "Paradise is surrounded by difficulties and Hell is surrounded by desires."[89] A person cannot attain Paradise without experiencing difficulties

---

86 Mālik, *k. wuqūt al-ṣalāh*, 6 and Al-Ṭaḥāwī, *Sharḥ Maʿāni al-Āthār*, 1:193 #1152

87 Tirmidhī, *k. al-ṣalāh, b. mā jā'a anna awwal mā yuḥāsab bihī al-ʿabd yawm al-qiyāmah al-ṣalāh*, 413

88 3:14 - زُيِّنَ لِلنَّاسِ حُبُّ الشَّهَوَاتِ مِنَ النِّسَاءِ وَالْبَنِينَ وَالْقَنَاطِيرِ الْمُقَنطَرَةِ مِنَ الذَّهَبِ وَالْفِضَّةِ وَالْخَيْلِ الْمُسَوَّمَةِ وَالْأَنْعَامِ وَالْحَرْثِ ذَٰلِكَ مَتَاعُ الْحَيَاةِ الدُّنْيَا وَاللَّهُ عِندَهُ حُسْنُ الْمَآبِ

89 Muslim, *k. al-jannah wa ṣifah naʿīmihā wa ahlihā*, 2822

and sacrifices, which include controlling and subduing one's desires. At the same time, Hellfire is earned by indulging in vain desires without any restraint or control.

Allah ﷻ concludes the verse by telling us that these people who neglected prayer and followed their desires, "are going to meet evil." The word "ghayy" literally means misguidance but it's also used to give the meaning of evil. Here it is referring to their punishment. They will be punished in the Hereafter with loss and disgrace because of their poor choices and actions. ibn Masʿūd رضي الله عنه narrated that there's a cave in Hell by the name of Ghayy, which has more punishments than all of the punishments of Hell combined. ibn ʿAbbās رضي الله عنه commented that even Hell itself seeks protection from Ghayy. Allah ﷻ has prepared it for habitual adulterers who persist in adultery, and for drunkards who don't give up drinking and for those who take interest and won't stop, for those who disobey their parents, those who give false testimony, and for a woman who declares someone else's child as her husband's.[90]

After mentioning their punishment, Allah ﷻ makes an exception. He gives them a sense of hope letting them know that regardless of what they've done they can repent. Through Allah's ﷻ infinite grace and mercy, if they turn back to Him ﷻ, seek forgiveness, and repent sincerely they can still attain success and salvation.

VERSE 60

إِلَّا مَن تَابَ وَءَامَنَ وَعَمِلَ صَٰلِحًا فَأُوْلَٰٓئِكَ يَدْخُلُونَ ٱلْجَنَّةَ وَلَا
يُظْلَمُونَ شَيْـًٔا

Except those who repent, believe, and do righteous deeds;

90 Qurṭubī, *al-Jāmiʿ fī Aḥkām al-Quran*, 13: 477

for they will enter Paradise and will not be wronged at all.

Allah's ﷻ mercy is infinite and limitless; it is literally beyond our imagination. Those who neglected prayer and followed desires are going to face the consequences of their poor choices "except those who repent, believe, and do righteous deeds." Allah ﷻ is describing those who sincerely turn to Him ﷻ in repentance, feeling remorse and regret for their poor choices, and asking for His ﷻ forgiveness for neglecting prayers and following their desires. And this repentance is real because it leads to them renewing their faith and trying their best to live a life of righteousness through good deeds.

Tawbah - repentance, wipes out everything that came before it as long as it's sincere. In order for tawbah to be sincere, we have to feel a sense of regret and remorse. Secondly, we have to ask for forgiveness for our sins and disobedience. Thirdly, we have to make a firm resolution to not return to that sin again. That's why the Prophet ﷺ told us, "One who repents from a sin is like one who has no sin at all."[91] Because of their belief, their deeds, and repentance, Allah ﷻ will enter them into Paradise. That is the greatest achievement, success, triumph, and victory.

The formula to get to Paradise is very easy and straightforward; belief + good deeds + repentance = Paradise, but that doesn't mean we don't have to work hard. The people of Paradise will be led to it with honor and dignity. When they reach its gates, they will be opened for them and they will be welcomed by Angels congratulating them. "And those who were mindful of their Lord will be led to Paradise in [successive] groups. When they arrive at its [already] open gates, its keepers will say, 'You are safe and secure! You have done well, so come in, to stay forever.'"[92]

"And will not be wronged at all." Meaning, their reward will not be decreased at all even though they didn't do much. They will get their reward in full and even more out of the grace and mercy of Allah ﷻ. Allah ﷻ now describes the Paradise that those who repent will enter with three things.

---

91 al-Bayhaqī, *Shuʿab al-Īmān*, 6780

92 وَسِيقَ الَّذِينَ اتَّقَوْا رَبَّهُمْ إِلَى الْجَنَّةِ زُمَرًا ۖ حَتَّىٰ إِذَا جَاءُوهَا وَفُتِحَتْ أَبْوَابُهَا وَقَالَ لَهُمْ خَزَنَتُهَا سَلَامٌ عَلَيْكُمْ طِبْتُمْ فَادْخُلُوهَا خَالِدِينَ - 39:73

VERSE 61

جَنَّـٰتِ عَـدْنٍ ٱلَّـتِى وَعَدَ ٱلرَّحْمَـٰنُ عِبَـادَهُۥ بِٱلْغَيْـبِ ۚ إِنَّـهُۥ كَانَ وَعْدُهُۥ مَأْتِيًّا

[They will be in] gardens of eternity that the Most Merciful has promised His servants in the unseen. Indeed, His promise will be fulfilled.

The righteous believers will be admitted into gardens of perpetual bliss, enjoyment, and pleasure, wherein they will reside for eternity. This is a promise from Allah ﷻ, the absolutely and infinitely most Merciful, with something that is hidden and concealed from our faculties of perception. Paradise is from the world of the unseen. Although we have never seen these gardens, we believe in their existence because of the strength of our īmān; because of our belief in Allah ﷻ. We know with absolute conviction and certainty that Allah ﷻ will fulfill His promise to His servants because Allah ﷻ does not break His promises. The first description of Paradise is that it's for eternity. Eternity is a very interesting and unique concept. It is very hard for us as human beings to really understand what it means because we are limited by time and space. We experience time through units of measurement such as seconds, minutes, hours, days, weeks, months, and years. Paradise is going to be forever!

VERSE 62

لَّا يَسْمَعُونَ فِيهَا لَغْوًا إِلَّا سَلَـٰمًا ۖ وَلَهُمْ رِزْقُهُمْ فِيهَا بُكْرَةً وَعَشِيًّا

There they will not hear any idle talk- only [greetings of] safety and security - and there they will have their provision morning and evening.

The word "laghw" means idle, absurd, frivolous, useless, or abusive speech. It is used to refer to things such as stories, fables, songs, and tales that bring no worthwhile benefit; they serve as a pastime and entertainment. They don't convey positive meanings or contain any morals, lessons, or reminders. It's speech that distracts our hearts, taking us away from the remembrance of Allah ﷻ, and doesn't provide anything beneficial. Speech that is idle and useless is completely antithetical to the ethos of Islam. As believers, we're supposed to engage in speech and conversations that are purposeful and beneficial. ibn ʿAbbās رضي الله عنه said, "Laghw refers to anything that is devoid of the remembrance of Allah ﷻ; meaning their speech in Paradise will be praising Allah ﷻ and extolling Him."[93]

Allah ﷻ is telling us that In Paradise there'll be no idle talk; there will be no speech that is useless, absurd, frivolous, or abusive. The residents of Paradise will only hear "[greetings of] safety and security." Whatever conversations they engage in and whatever they hear in Paradise will add to their happiness, contentment, and peace. This includes the greeting of salām and the greeting of the Angels. The hearts of the people of Paradise will be pure and because of that, their speech will be good and pure. The tongue is the interpreter of the heart. There will be no hurtful, upsetting, offensive, or provocative speech.

93 Qurṭubī, *al-Jāmiʿ fī Aḥkām al-Quran*, 13:478

The people of Paradise will visit one another in amazing gatherings where they'll remember their lives in this world and how Allah ﷻ blessed them by granting them Paradise. "And We will remove whatever is in their breasts of resentment, [so they will be] brothers, on thrones facing each other."[94] In other places, Allah ﷻ describes some of the conversations that they'll have. "They will turn to one another inquisitively. They will say, 'Before [this reward] we used to be in awe [of Allah] in the midst of our people. So Allah has graced us and protected us from the torment of [Hell's] scorching heat. Indeed, we used to call upon Him [alone] before. He is truly the Most Kind, Most Merciful.'"[95]

"And there they will have their provision morning and evening." Meaning the people of paradise will get whatever they want - food, drink, and literally whatever their hearts desire - morning and evening. There's no solar system in Paradise so there'll be no rising or setting of the sun, but there will be a perpetual radiance. However, there will be some way to differentiate between night and day. Whatever they want they'll get, "For them is whatever they desire."

Paradise is that place in which there are things that no eye has ever seen, no ear has ever heard, and things that haven't even been imagined.[96] The delights of Paradise go beyond our imagination and can't be described. "It's a sparkling light, aromatic plants, a lofty palace, a flowing river, ripe fruit, a beautiful wife and abundant clothing, an eternal abode of radiant joy, in beautiful strong houses."[97]

The buildings of paradise are made of, "bricks of gold and silver, and mortar of fragrant musk, pebbles of pearl and sapphire, and soil of saffron. Whoever enters it is filled with joy and will never feel miserable; he will live there forever and will never die. Their clothes will never wear out and their youth will never fade."[98] Paradise is enclosed by eight gates that will be opened for them. One gate is for those who fasted, another for those who prayed, another for those who gave charity and another for those who strug-

94 وَنَزَعْنَا مَا فِي صُدُورِهِم مِّنْ غِلٍّ إِخْوَانًا عَلَىٰ سُرُرٍ مُّتَقَابِلِينَ - 15:47

95 وَأَقْبَلَ بَعْضُهُمْ عَلَىٰ بَعْضٍ يَتَسَاءَلُونَ * قَالُوا إِنَّا كُنَّا قَبْلُ فِي أَهْلِنَا مُشْفِقِينَ * فَمَنَّ اللَّهُ عَلَيْنَا وَوَقَانَا عَذَابَ السَّمُومِ * إِنَّا كُنَّا مِن قَبْلُ نَدْعُوهُ ۖ إِنَّهُ هُوَ الْبَرُّ الرَّحِيمُ - 52:25-28

96 Bukhārī, *k. bad' al-khalq b. mā jā' fī ṣifah al-jannah wa annahā makhlūqah*, 3244 and Muslim, 2842b

97 Ibn Mājah, *k. al-zuhd b. ṣifah al-jannah*, 4332

98 Aḥmad, *Musnad*, 2:304 #8030

gled in the path of Allah ﷻ. The Prophet ﷺ told us, "Whoever performs wuḍū and does it well, then says that I bear witness that there's nobody worthy of worship except Allah and that Muḥammad is the servant of Allah and His Messenger, the eight gates of Paradise will be opened for them and they can enter through any of them they want."[99] These gates are so big that the distance between the two gate panels is that of a forty-year journey.

The soil of Paradise is made of a fine white powder of pure musk. The rivers in Paradise are surrounded by banks of pearls and musk. One river is described as "its banks are made of pearls and rubies. The soil it flows over is more fragrant than musk. And its water is sweeter than honey and whiter than milk."[100] There are rivers of water, milk, wine, and clear honey. "In it are rivers of fresh water, rivers of milk that never changes in taste, rivers of wine delicious to drink, and rivers of pure honey. There they will ⌜also⌝ have all kinds of fruit, and forgiveness from their Lord."[101]

The homes of Paradise are built from bricks of gold and silver. There are these magnificent pavilions built from pearls. Each one is made out of a hollowed pearl that is sixty miles high and sixty miles wide. One of the ways of being rewarded with these homes in Paradise is by participating in the construction of masājid (mosques) in this world. The Prophet ﷺ said, "Whoever builds a mosque for the sake of Allah, then Allah will build them a home in Paradise."[102]

The Prophet ﷺ said, "The first batch to enter Paradise will appear like the moon of a night that it is full. They do not spit, nor do their noses run, nor do they defecate. Their vessels are of gold, their combs are of silver and gold, their perfume is of Aluwwah, and their sweat is musk. Each one of them has two wives, so beautiful that the marrow of their shins can be seen through the flesh. There is no differing among them nor mutual hatred, and their hearts are like the heart of one man, and they glorify Allah morning and evening."[103]

---

99 Muslim, *k. al-ṭahārah, b. al-dhikr al-musṭaḥab ʿaqib al-wuḍū*, 234

100 Bukhārī, *k. al-raqāʾiq b. fī al-ḥawḍ*, 6581 and Aḥmad, *Musnad*, #13156

101 47:15 - فِيهَا أَنْهَارٌ مِّن مَّاءٍ غَيْرِ آسِنٍ وَأَنْهَارٌ مِّن لَّبَنٍ لَّمْ يَتَغَيَّرْ طَعْمُهُ وَأَنْهَارٌ مِّنْ خَمْرٍ لَّذَّةٍ لِّلشَّارِبِينَ وَأَنْهَارٌ مِّنْ عَسَلٍ مُّصَفًّى وَلَهُمْ فِيهَا مِن كُلِّ الثَّمَرَاتِ وَمَغْفِرَةٌ مِّن رَّبِّهِمْ

102 Muslim, *k. al-masājid wa mawāḍiʿ al-ṣalāh, b. faḍl binā al-masājid wa al-hath ʿalayhā*, 533

103 Tirmidhī, *k. ṣifah al-jannah ʿan rasūlillah*, 2733

There's no comparison between the life of this world and the life to come. The Prophet ﷺ explained this to us saying, "By Allah, this world in comparison to the Hereafter is nothing more than as if one of you put his finger (and he gestured with his forefinger) in the sea: let him see how much water he would retrieve."[104] The clothing, food, drink, jewelry and houses of the people of Paradise are unimaginable. There's no comparison. The smallest space in Paradise is better than this world and everything that it contains. "The space of a whip in Paradise is better than this world and everything in it."

VERSE 63

تِلْكَ ٱلْجَنَّةُ ٱلَّتِى نُورِثُ مِنْ عِبَادِنَا مَن كَانَ تَقِيًّا

That is Paradise, which We give as inheritance to those of Our servants who feared Allah.

This absolutely amazing, unimaginable place that has been described in very illustrative and various ways throughout the Quran is Paradise that will be given as inheritance to the people of taqwā, God-consciousness. Allah ﷻ is telling us that one of the most important keys for achieving eternal salvation in the Hereafter is the quality or characteristic of taqwā. Those individuals who were mindful, conscious, and aware of Allah ﷻ, both in public and in private, by trying their best to obey His commands and stay away from His prohibitions, will be granted Paradise. As Allah ﷻ says in Sūrah al-Mu'minūn, "Successful indeed are the believers: those who humble themselves in prayer; those who avoid idle talk; those who

104 Muslim, *k. al-jannah wa ṣifah naʿīmihā wa ahlihā, b. fanā al-dunya wa bayān al-hashr yawm al-qiyāmah,* 2858

pay zakāh; those who guard their chastity except with their spouses or their slaves—with these they are not to blame, but whoever seeks beyond that are the transgressors; ⌜the believers are also⌝ those who are true to their trusts and covenants; and those who are ⌜properly⌝ observant of their prayers. Those are the inheritors who will inherit Firdaus (the Paradise). They will be there forever."[105] Allah ﷻ also says in Sūrah Āl ʿImrān, "And hasten towards forgiveness from your Lord and a Paradise as vast as the heavens and the earth, prepared for those mindful [of Allah]."[106]

LESSONS AND BENEFITS FROM VERSES 59-63

1.

Concern for Future Generations - As believers, one of our primary concerns should be our spiritual health; our relationship with Allah ﷻ. We are supposed to work on nurturing and protecting faith within our hearts, allowing it to grow and blossom so that it expresses itself through our speech, behavior, and character. We should have this deep concern for our īmān and our salvation in the life to come. Just as we have this concern for ourselves, we should also have it for our families; spouses, children, parents, and relatives. We should have this concern for the entire community and future generations. There should be genuine care and concern for the protection of faith and religion in society. This was the concern of all Prophets and Messengers and was highlighted specifically in the story of Zakariyyā ﷺ mentioned earlier. Allah ﷻ says in Sūrah al-Taḥrīm, "O believers! Protect yourselves and your families from a Fire whose fuel is people and stones, overseen by formidable and severe angels, who never disobey whatever Allah orders—always

105 قَدْ أَفْلَحَ الْمُؤْمِنُونَ * الَّذِينَ هُمْ فِي صَلَاتِهِمْ خَاشِعُونَ * وَالَّذِينَ هُمْ عَنِ اللَّغْوِ مُعْرِضُونَ * وَالَّذِينَ هُمْ لِلزَّكَاةِ فَاعِلُونَ * وَالَّذِينَ هُمْ لِفُرُوجِهِمْ حَافِظُونَ * إِلَّا عَلَىٰ أَزْوَاجِهِمْ أَوْ مَا مَلَكَتْ أَيْمَانُهُمْ فَإِنَّهُمْ غَيْرُ مَلُومِينَ * فَمَنِ ابْتَغَىٰ وَرَاءَ ذَٰلِكَ فَأُولَٰئِكَ هُمُ الْعَادُونَ * وَالَّذِينَ هُمْ لِأَمَانَاتِهِمْ وَعَهْدِهِمْ رَاعُونَ * وَالَّذِينَ هُمْ عَلَىٰ صَلَوَاتِهِمْ يُحَافِظُونَ * أُولَٰئِكَ هُمُ الْوَارِثُونَ * الَّذِينَ يَرِثُونَ الْفِرْدَوْسَ هُمْ فِيهَا خَالِدُونَ - 23:1-11

106 وَسَارِعُوا إِلَىٰ مَغْفِرَةٍ مِّن رَّبِّكُمْ وَجَنَّةٍ عَرْضُهَا السَّمَاوَاتُ وَالْأَرْضُ أُعِدَّتْ لِلْمُتَّقِينَ - 3:133

doing as commanded."[107]

2.

Controlling Desires - Desires are an extremely powerful force that take us away from our true purpose in life. The Prophet ﷺ said, "The intelligent person is one who subdues his lower self and works for what comes after death. The unintelligent person is one who allows his soul to follow its desires and then has [false] hopes in Allah."[108]

3.

Importance of Prayer

4.

Repentance

5.

Formula for Success - Īmān + Righteous Deeds = Paradise

6.

The Promise of Allah ﷻ - Allah's ﷻ promise always comes true.

7.

The Centrality of Taqwā

In the last passage, Allah ﷻ described the generations of people who came after their Prophets and Messengers, those who slowly moved away from their teachings, neglected prayer, and started following their desires. Allah ﷻ warned them that because of their neglect of prayer and following of desires they will face punishment in the Hereafter. Then, He ﷻ mentioned an exception, those who believe, repent, and do righteous deeds will be saved from punishment and will enter Paradise. In the next verse, Allah ﷻ addresses the Prophet ﷺ directly as somewhat of a conclusion to the previous subjects and discussions.

---

107 يَا أَيُّهَا الَّذِينَ آمَنُوا قُوا أَنفُسَكُمْ وَأَهْلِيكُمْ نَارًا وَقُودُهَا النَّاسُ وَالْحِجَارَةُ عَلَيْهَا مَلَائِكَةٌ غِلَاظٌ شِدَادٌ لَّا يَعْصُونَ اللَّهَ مَا أَمَرَهُمْ وَيَفْعَلُونَ مَا يُؤْمَرُونَ - 66:6

108 Tirmidhī, *k. ṣifah al-qiyāmah wa al-raqā'iq wa al-war' 'an rasūlillah*, 2459

VERSE 64

وَمَا نَتَنَزَّلُ إِلَّا بِأَمْرِ رَبِّكَ ۖ لَهُۥ مَا بَيْنَ أَيْدِينَا وَمَا خَلْفَنَا وَمَا
بَيْنَ ذَٰلِكَ ۚ وَمَا كَانَ رَبُّكَ نَسِيًّا

We only descend by the command of your Lord. To Him belongs whatever is before us, and whatever is behind us, and everything in between. And your Lord is never forgetful.

This verse has a specific background or context in which it was revealed. It was revealed in response to a question that the Prophet ﷺ posed to Jibrīl عليه السلام. ibn ʿAbbās رضي الله عنه narrated that the Messenger of Allah ﷺ asked Jibrīl عليه السلام, "What prevents you from visiting us more often?"

In response, this particular verse was revealed, where Allah ﷻ mentions Jibrīl's ﷺ response. "We only descend by the command of your Lord. To Him belongs whatever is before us, and whatever is behind us, and everything in between. And your Lord is never forgetful." [109]

In another narration, we learn why the Prophet ﷺ asked Jibrīl ﷺ this question. Based on information from the Rabbis of Madinah, the non-believers of Quraysh asked the Prophet ﷺ about the story of the People of the Cave, Dhū al-Qarnain, and the soul. The Prophet ﷺ responded saying that he would give them the answer tomorrow, but he forgot to say in shā' Allah, if Allah wills. Because of this slight oversight, Allah ﷻ delayed revelation and didn't send Jibrīl ﷺ with the answer for fifteen days. These fifteen days were extremely difficult upon the Prophet ﷺ. He didn't know how to answer, and the people of Quraysh took that as an opportunity to mock and ridicule him. When Jibrīl ﷺ was sent with the answer, the Prophet ﷺ said, "O Jibrīl! You didn't come to me and I started getting worried and longed for you." Jibrīl ﷺ responded, "I longed for you as well, but I'm a commanded servant. If I'm sent I come and if I'm stopped I stay."[110]

Through this question, the Prophet ﷺ was expressing his love for Jibrīl ﷺ and his anticipation for receiving revelation from Allah ﷻ. He ﷺ would look forward to receiving revelation from Allah ﷻ. Allah ﷻ told Jibrīl ﷺ to say, "We only descend by the command of your Lord." Meaning, the Angels don't come down to the Prophets and Messengers with revelation except when Allah ﷻ commands them to, according to His divine wisdom and what He ﷻ deems as beneficial for them in this life and the next. The Angels descend and come to this world when Allah ﷻ tells them to, according to His divine decree and wisdom. The reasoning behind this is because Allah ﷻ knows best when to send His Angels; His knowledge is perfect and all encompassing.

"To Him belongs whatever is before us, and whatever is behind us, and everything in between." According to ibn ʿAbbās ؓ "whatever is before us" refers to what happened in the life of this world, "whatever is behind us" refers to the life of the Hereafter, and "everything in between" refers to the period of life in between death and the Day of Judgment known as barzakh.[111] Qa-

109 Bukhārī, *k. bad' al-khalq, b. dhikr al-malā'ikah*, 3218

110 Rāzī, *Tafsīr al-Rāzī*, 21:239

111 Qurṭubī, *al-Jāmiʿ lī Aḥkām al-Quran*, 13:482

tādah says that "whatever is before us" refers to the Hereafter, "whatever is behind us" refers to the life of this world, and "everything in between" refers to the time in between the two soundings of the Horn.[112] al-Akhfash says that "whatever is before us" refers to what happened before we were created, "whatever is behind us" refers to what happens after we die, and "everything in between" refers to what happens between our creation and death. Literally every single thing in this universe - big and small, old and young, secret and public, known and unknown, animate and inanimate - belongs to Allah. He alone is the King and Sovereign of this entire universe and everything it contains, which includes time; the past, present, and future. He created it, sustains it, and controls it through His infinite might, power, knowledge, wisdom, and authority. He alone is the One who is in charge and in control of the system of the universe, the affairs of this world and the next, all places, directions, times, past, present, and future. Part of that which belongs to Him is revelation and when to send it down.

"And your Lord is never forgetful." Through this portion of the verse, Allah is consoling, comforting, and reassuring the Prophet. Allah hasn't forgotten or forsaken you, even though revelation may have been delayed for a short time. Rather, this delay is based on some deep divine wisdom for a particular benefit that may or may not be understood.

VERSE 65

رَّبُّ ٱلسَّمَٰوَٰتِ وَٱلْأَرْضِ وَمَا بَيْنَهُمَا فَٱعْبُدْهُ وَٱصْطَبِرْ لِعِبَٰدَتِهِۦ ۚ هَلْ
تَعْلَمُ لَهُۥ سَمِيًّا

[He is] the Lord of the heavens, and the earth, and every-

112 Qurṭubī, *al-Jāmiʿ lī Aḥkām al-Quran*, 13:482

thing in between. So worship Him and be steadfast in His worship. Do you know of anyone equal to Him?

In this verse, Allah ﷻ is describing Himself as the Lord, Master, Creator, Nourisher, and Cherisher of the heavens and the earth and whatever's between them; this entire universe and whatever it contains. He alone is al-Rabb. He ﷻ alone is the One who has complete knowledge, control, sovereignty, and authority over this world and everything that it contains. Not a single leaf falls from a tree without the will and permission of Allah ﷻ and not a single leaf turns as it falls without the will and permission of Allah ﷻ. So worship Allah ﷻ alone, sincerely, without any partners.

"And be steadfast in His worship." Remain firm, strong, consistent, and steadfast upon worship. The verb used here gives an exaggerated meaning of patient perseverance. Meaning, no matter what's going on, no matter how difficult things may seem, remain extremely consistent in your obedience and worship. Patience and steadfastness are central components of our worship, obedience, and servitude to Allah ﷻ. Oftentimes there are certain hardships and difficulties associated with praying, fasting, giving charity, treating others well, and dealing with the various challenges of life. During times of sadness and difficulty, the Prophet ﷺ is being advised to remain patient and turn towards Allah ﷻ in worship. The same thing applies for us.

"Do you know of anyone equal to Him?" This is a rhetorical question, a literary device often used to emphasize a certain point. Meaning, there's nothing that resembles or is similar to Allah ﷻ in any way, shape, or form. There's absolutely nothing like Him.

LESSONS AND BENEFITS FROM VERSES 64-65

1.

The infinite might, power, magnificence, and glory of Allah ﷻ.

2.

The infinite knowledge and wisdom of Allah ﷻ.

3.

Steadfastness in worship.

4.

Allah ﷻ is absolutely unique.

From here, Allah ﷻ changes the subject of the Sūrah. So far, the Sūrah has primarily focused on the concepts of tawḥīd and messengership. In the next passage, the Sūrah focuses on the concept of life after death. Allah ﷻ addresses some of the doubts the non-believers of Makkah had regarding resurrection, life after death, and judgment.

VERSE 66

وَيَقُولُ ٱلْإِنسَـٰنُ أَءِذَا مَا مِتُّ لَسَوْفَ أُخْرَجُ حَيًّا

And man says, "After I die, will I really be brought back to life again?"

This verse was revealed regarding the likes of Ubay ibn Khalaf and al-Walīd ibn al-Mughīrah and those similar to them. They were sworn enemies of the Prophet ﷺ and found the idea of resurrection and life after death to be ridiculous and far-fetched. It's narrated that Ubay ibn Khalaf picked up an old, dry, brittle bone and crushed it in his hand saying, "Muḥammad believes that we will be resurrected after death."[113] The "man" in the verse is referring to these two men and anyone else who holds the same beliefs and attitude.

"After I die, will I really be brought back to life again?" This is a statement of disbelief and amazement mixed with mockery, sarcasm, and ridicule. He's rhetorically asking the Prophet ﷺ, "When I die and my body turns into dust, will I really be brought back to life from my grave and held accountable for my deeds?" He and those similar to him found the concept of life after death to be extremely far-fetched and nonsensical. This attitude and the response to it is mentioned elsewhere in the Quran as well. For example, Allah ﷻ says in Sūrah al-Raʿd, "[Now,] if anything should amaze you [O Prophet], then it is their question: 'When we are reduced to dust, will we really be raised as a new creation?'"[114] Similarly, Allah ﷻ says in Sūrah Yāsīn, "Do people not see that We have created them from a sperm-drop, then—behold!—they openly challenge [Us]? And they argue with Us—forgetting they were created—saying, 'Who will give life to decayed bones?' Say, [O Prophet,] 'They will be revived by the One Who produced them the first time, for He has [perfect] knowledge of every created being.'"[115]

As a response to this disbelief and sarcasm, Allah ﷻ reminds them of His infinite might and power, particularly His ability to bring the dead back to life, with a very simple rational argument.

113 Qurṭubī, *al-Jāmiʿ lī Aḥkām al-Quran*, 13:485

114 وَإِن تَعْجَبْ فَعَجَبٌ قَوْلُهُمْ أَإِذَا كُنَّا تُرَابًا أَإِنَّا لَفِي خَلْقٍ جَدِيدٍ - 13:5

115 أَوَلَمْ يَرَ الْإِنسَانُ أَنَّا خَلَقْنَاهُ مِن نُّطْفَةٍ فَإِذَا هُوَ خَصِيمٌ مُّبِينٌ * وَضَرَبَ لَنَا مَثَلًا وَنَسِيَ خَلْقَهُ قَالَ مَن يُحْيِي الْعِظَامَ وَهِيَ رَمِيمٌ * قُلْ يُحْيِيهَا الَّذِي أَنشَأَهَا أَوَّلَ مَرَّةٍ وَهُوَ بِكُلِّ خَلْقٍ عَلِيمٌ - 36:77-79

VERSE 67

أَوَلَا يَذْكُرُ ٱلْإِنسَـٰنُ أَنَّا خَلَقْنَـٰهُ مِن قَبْلُ وَلَمْ يَكُ شَيْـًٔا

Does man not remember that We created him before, when he was nothing?

This is a rhetorical question meant to really drive the point home and get them to start thinking about Allah's might and power. Doesn't man remember how he was created from nothing? How he was brought from non-existence to existence? Why doesn't he reflect on his own origin and creation? If Allah ﷻ has the ability to create something from nothing, then re-creating it is much easier. As Allah ﷻ says in Sūrah al-Rūm, "And it is He who begins creation; then He repeats it, and that is [even] easier for Him."[116] In a ḥadīth qudsī, Allah ﷻ says, "The son of Adam denied Me and he had no right to do so. And the son of Adam reviled Me and he had no right to do so. As for his denying Me, it is his saying that I will not resurrect him as I created him in the beginning, but resurrecting him is not more difficult for Me than creating him in the first place. And as for his reviling Me, it is his saying that Allah has taken a son, but I am Allah, the One, the Self-Sufficient Master, I beget not nor was I begotten, and there is none co-equal or comparable unto Me."[117]

Allah ﷻ then warns and threatens those who refuse to believe in life after death.

116 وَهُوَ الَّذِي يَبْدَأُ الْخَلْقَ ثُمَّ يُعِيدُهُ وَهُوَ أَهْوَنُ عَلَيْهِ - 30:27

117 Bukhārī, *k. al-tafsīr*, 4974

VERSE 68

فَوَرَبِّكَ لَنَحْشُرَنَّهُمْ وَٱلشَّيَـٰطِينَ ثُمَّ لَنُحْضِرَنَّهُمْ حَوْلَ جَهَنَّمَ جِثِيًّا

By your Lord, We will surely gather them along with the devils; and then set them around Hell on their knees.

This is a very powerful and emphatic statement. The "wāw" at the beginning of the verse is known as "wāw al-qasm," or the wāw of an oath. Allah ﷻ is swearing by Himself saying, "By your Lord." An oath is usually taken to highlight the truthfulness, importance, and weight of something. The thing that is sworn by is also usually something very important or valuable. Imagine, Allah ﷻ, the Lord of the worlds, is swearing by Himself, saying, "We will surely gather them along with the devils." Meaning, without a doubt, we will resurrect them, bring them back to life, raise them from their graves, and gather all of them together on the plain of resurrection along with the devils that deceived and misguided them.

"And then set them around Hell on their knees." On the Day of Resurrection, every single person, from the beginning of time till the end of time, believers and non-believers, fortunate and the unfortunate, will be gathered and brought to the plain of resurrection. The non-believers will be assembled around Hell on their knees. They will be overcome with this intense feeling of fear, horror, and regret, causing them to fall on their knees. As Allah ﷻ says in Sūrah al-Jāthiyah, "And you will see every faith-community on its knees."[118] Then the believers and the blessed will be taken across Hell and granted entry into Paradise.

118 وَتَرَىٰ كُلَّ أُمَّةٍ جَاثِيَةً - 45:28

VERSE 69

ثُمَّ لَنَنزِعَنَّ مِن كُلِّ شِيعَةٍ أَيُّهُمْ أَشَدُّ عَلَى ٱلرَّحْمَـٰنِ عِتِيًّا

Then, out of every group, We will certainly draw out those who were more rebellious against the All-Merciful.

At this moment, all of the non-believers are on their knees, gathered around Hell, this wild raging fire, full of fear, horror, and terror. Allah ﷻ will seize those from every religious nation or community that were the most severe in disobedience to Him - those that had the most pride and arrogance, those who ignored the limits set by Allah ﷻ, and led others astray as well.

VERSE 70

ثُمَّ لَنَحْنُ أَعْلَمُ بِٱلَّذِينَ هُمْ أَوْلَىٰ بِهَا صِلِيًّا

And We truly know best who is most deserving of burning in it.

This is another threat and warning to the non-believers. Allah ﷻ is aware and knows who deserves to be punished in the fire of Hell. Allah ﷻ is al-ʿAlīm, the All-Knowing, and al-Khabīr, the All-Aware. He knows every single thing - big or small, private and public, seen and unseen. He ﷻ is fully aware of what people conceal in their hearts and what people expose; what their eyes steal and what their chests conceal. He ﷻ knows best who's deserving of punishment and who is not.

VERSE 71

وَإِن مِّنكُمْ إِلَّا وَارِدُهَا ۚ كَانَ عَلَىٰ رَبِّكَ حَتْمًا مَّقْضِيًّا

And every single one of you will approach it, a decree from your Lord which must be fulfilled.

This is an extremely frightening and terrifying statement from Allah ﷻ that should fill our hearts with fear and cause our skin to crawl. He's telling us that every single person, believer and non-believer, righteous and sinner, will be brought close to Hellfire and made to approach it. Everyone will be made to go across Hellfire. From several narrations of the Prophet ﷺ, we learn that there's a bridge across Hell known as al-Ṣirāṭ. In a ḥadīth it has been described as being thinner than a strand of hair and sharper than the blade of a sword.[119] Everyone will cross this bridge, and according to his or her beliefs and actions, they will cross it differently. This is something that has been decreed and decided by Allah ﷻ.[120]

ibn Masʿūd رضي الله عنه narrated that he heard the Prophet ﷺ say, "Everyone will

---

119 Muslim, *k. al-īmān, b. maʿrifah ṭarīq al-ru'yah,* 183

120 ibn Kathīr, *al-Bidāyah wa al-Nihāyah,* 2:91

cross the bridge and will be taken across according to their deeds. Some will pass across it like lightning, some like wind, some like birds, some like the best horses, some like the best camels, some like the running of a man, until the last to cross will be a man whose light is only on his big toes, and he too will pass. The Ṣirāṭ is extremely slippery, it's surrounded by thorns and there are Angels on its sides with dogs from Hell who grab people."

Abū Hurayrah 🙼 narrates that the Messenger of Allah 🙼 said, "Amānah (trust) and ties of kinship will be sent forth and will stand on both sides of the Ṣirāṭ, the right and left. The first of you will then pass [across it] like lightning." Abū Hurayrah 🙼 said, "May my father and mother be ransomed for you, what is like the movement of lightning?" The Messenger of Allah 🙼 replied, "Have you not seen how lightning comes and goes in the blink of an eye? Then (the next group will pass) like the breeze, then like a bird and a running man; they will move according to the quality of their deeds. (During this time) your Prophet 🙼 will remain standing on the Bridge saying, 'My Lord! Keep (them) safe, keep (them) safe.' Then a man's deeds will be so weak that they will only be able to crawl [across the bridge]. There are long hooks on both sides of the Bridge, ordered to snatch those they are told to. Some will escape with lacerations and others will be thrown into the Fire." Abū Hurayrah added, "By Him in Whose Hand is Abū Hurayrah's soul, the pit of Hell is seventy years deep."[121]

The Messenger of Allah 🙼 also said, "A Muslim whose three children die (in infancy) will not enter the Fire except for the fulfillment of Allah's oath."[122] Allah's oath in this ḥadīth refers to His statement, "And every single one of you will approach it, a decree from your Lord which must be fulfilled."

This verse affected the attitude of the righteous and kept them awake at night. It changed their whole life and kept them from laughing and enjoying their pleasures excessively. ibn Kathīr 🙼 mentions that when Abū Maysarah went to bed he said, "Would that my mother had never given birth to me!" Then he wept. He was asked, "Why are you weeping, O Abū Maysarah?" He said, "Allah has told us that we will pass over it (Hell), but He has not told us that we will be saved from falling into it." [123]

---

121   Muslim, *k. al-īmān, b. adnā ahl al-jannah manzilah fīhā*, 195

122   Bukhārī, *k. al-īmān wa al-nudhūr, b. qawl Allah wa aqsamu billAh jahd aymānihim*, 6656

123   ibn Kathīr, *Tafsīr al-Quran al-ʿAẓīm*,

VERSE 72

ثُمَّ نُنَجِّى ٱلَّذِينَ ٱتَّقَوا۟ وَّنَذَرُ ٱلظَّٰلِمِينَ فِيهَا جِثِيًّا

Then We will save those who feared Allah and leave the wrongdoers within it, on their knees.

Meaning, as people are crossing the Bridge over Hell, Allah ﷾ will save and deliver the people of taqwā. Allah ﷾ will save those who were mindful, conscious, and aware of Him to the best of their abilities, by obeying His commands and staying away from His prohibitions. As for the wrongdoers, Allah ﷾ will allow them to be snatched and pulled off the Bridge, falling into the Fire, where they will reside for eternity. This applies specifically to the non-believers. As for the wrongdoers among the believers, then they are under the will of Allah ﷾. If Allah ﷾ wills, He can forgive them and pardon them through His infinite grace and mercy. And if He ﷾ wills, He can hold them accountable through His infinite justice, and then admit them to Paradise after they have paid their dues.

LESSONS AND BENEFITS FROM VERSES 66-72

1.

Life after death is an absolute certainty. An intelligent person should spend their time, energy, efforts, and wealth preparing for the Last Day through īmān, righteous deeds, forgiveness, repentance, and reliance upon Allah ﷾.

2.

The reality and certainty of life after death is understood through very simple and straightforward rational and observational proofs.

3.

The Day of Judgment is going to be frightening.

4.

Taqwā is the path to salvation. When the Prophet ﷺ was asked what is the quickest way to Paradise he said, "Being mindful of Allah and good character."[124]

5.

Ẓulm is the path to damnation. The Prophet ﷺ said, "Ẓulm will be [layers] of darkness on the Day of Judgment."[125]

---

124 Tirmidhī, *k. al-birr wa al-ṣilah ʿan rasūlillah, b. mā jā'a fī ḥusn al-khuluq*, 2004

125 Bukhārī, *k. al-maẓālim, b. al-ẓulm ẓulumāt yawm al-qiyāmah*, 2447

In the next set of verses, Allah ﷻ responds to another doubt that the people of Quraysh had posed to the Prophet ﷺ and his Companions. The Polytheists of Makkah believed that their wealth, power, and status was a sign of divine favor and blessing; that if Allah ﷻ were displeased and angry with them, then He wouldn't have given them so much material wealth and power. In contrast, the Muslims were poor and weak, which meant that Allah ﷻ must not be pleased with them. If what the Muslims claim is true, then the situation should be the exact opposite. Basically, their wealth and power had gotten to their heads; it made them proud and arrogant, blinding them from accepting the truth. Allah ﷻ responds by reminding them about the fate of past nations and communities that had adopted the same attitude of arrogance and pride. Allah ﷻ says,

VERSE 73

وَإِذَا تُتْلَىٰ عَلَيْهِمْ ءَايَٰتُنَا بَيِّنَٰتٍ قَالَ ٱلَّذِينَ كَفَرُوا۟ لِلَّذِينَ ءَامَنُوٓا۟

أَىُّ ٱلْفَرِيقَيْنِ خَيْرٌ مَّقَامًا وَأَحْسَنُ نَدِيًّا

And when Our verses are recited to them in all their clarity, those who disbelieve say to those who believe, "Which of the two groups is better in status and superior in assembly?"

In this verse, Allah ﷻ is presenting an objection or doubt of the Mushrikūn (polytheists) of Makkah. The Prophet ﷺ, as part of his mission and effort, would recite the verses of the Quran to the Mushrikūn of Makkah. Oftentimes, he would be met with opposition, rejection, mockery, ridicule, and derision. Allah ﷻ is telling us that when the verses of the Quran are recited to the Mushrikūn as clear evidence of the existence and oneness of Allah ﷻ, as clear proof that Muḥammad ﷺ is the last and final Messenger, and as proof that life after death is a reality, they turn away in arrogance and pride. They respond to the believers by saying, "Which of the two groups is better in status and superior in assembly?" Meaning, they ask in mockery and arrogance, which of us is in a better position materially? Who has more wealth, power, strength, and status? Who has more supporters and followers? You or us?

Remember, this Sūrah was revealed during the early Makkan period of Prophethood, when most of the people who had accepted Islam were poor and weak. The Mushrikūn are arguing that if the Muslims are upon the truth, and they themselves are in the wrong, then the condition of the Muslims in this world should be much better. They should be the ones who are rich, powerful, wealthy, and influential. But, since the opposite is true, it means that we're upon the truth and they're wrong. The Quraysh literally tried everything they could to argue against the Muslims. It's a common theme throughout history, that wealth and power cause people to be proud and arrogant to such an extent that even the wise and sensible are led to believe that their prosperity will last forever. Allah ﷻ responds to this false perception of reality by saying,

VERSE 74

وَكَمْ أَهْلَكْنَا قَبْلَهُم مِّن قَرْنٍ هُمْ أَحْسَنُ أَثَـٰثًا وَرِءْيًا

And how many generations have We destroyed before them, who were better in assets and splendour?

Allah ﷻ is drawing the attention of the Mushrikūn of Makkah towards past nations and communities that were destroyed because of their arrogance and rejection of the truth. These nations and communities were even more materially blessed than the Makkans; they had more wealth, assets, properties, power, strength, beauty, and authority. Look at how many generations of people have been destroyed before you - who had more wealth, power, and beauty than you - because of their disbelief and rejection of their messengers. Their wealth, power, influence, and authority didn't save them or protect them from the punishment of Allah ﷻ.

Allah ﷻ is drawing their attention towards history, especially of those nations that they were aware of such as, ʿĀd and Thamūd. Allah ﷻ responds to their doubt and objection by reminding them that material wealth doesn't necessarily mean that a nation is being favored by Allah ﷻ. History is full of instances where rich and powerful nations were reduced to dust and vanished without leaving a trace because of their disbelief and rejection of the truth. Material wealth and prosperity aren't signs of Allah's ﷻ love and approval, and poverty is not a sign of Allah's ﷻ displeasure and disapproval. Both prosperity and poverty are tests from Allah ﷻ; prosperity is test of gratitude and poverty is a test of patience.

Allah ﷻ then warns them and reminds them that they will face punishment without a doubt, either in this world or the next.

VERSE 75

قُلْ مَن كَانَ فِى ٱلضَّلَٰلَةِ فَلْيَمْدُدْ لَهُ ٱلرَّحْمَٰنُ مَدًّا ۚ حَتَّىٰٓ إِذَا رَأَوْا۟
مَا يُوعَدُونَ إِمَّا ٱلْعَذَابَ وَإِمَّا ٱلسَّاعَةَ فَسَيَعْلَمُونَ مَنْ هُوَ شَرٌّ
مَّكَانًا وَأَضْعَفُ جُندًا

Say, "Whoever is [entrenched] in misguidance, the Most Merciful will allow them plenty of time, until they see what they have been warned about: either the punishment or the Hour - they will realize who is worse in position and inferior in manpower."

In this verse, Allah ﷻ is addressing the Prophet ﷺ directly. O Prophet! Warn the Mushrikūn and let them know that those who are misguided thinking they're on the truth; Allah ﷻ leaves them upon misguidance. He lets them enjoy this world, granting them wealth and pleasure, gives them respite, and allows them to sink deeper and deeper into darkness. The scholars term this phenomenon istidrāj. Istidrāj is "'being taken to perdition in small, unnoticeable degrees', which occurs for a corrupt sinful person (fāsiq) or disbeliever (kāfir), in correspondence to his wishes, due to the divine plotting against him, such that the person is distracted with his gifts and therefore forgets to repent."[126] This has been the way of Allah ﷻ with the wrongdoers and sinners throughout history. Allah ﷻ says in Sūrah Āl 'Imrān, "Those who disbelieve should not think that living longer is good for them. They are only given more time to increase in sin, and they will suffer a

126 Khan, *An Introduction to Islamic Theology*, 197

humiliating punishment."[127] Similarly, in Sūrah al-Anʿām, Allah ﷻ says, "We turn their hearts and eyes away [from the truth] as they refused to believe at first, leaving them to wander blindly in their defiance." [128]

Allah ﷻ is telling us that they will be allowed to sink deeper and deeper into misguidance and darkness until they see what they've been promised; either punishment in this world, or punishment in the world to come. Once they see what they have been promised with their own two eyes, they'll "realize who is worse in position and inferior in manpower." They'll recognize the real truth, but it will be too late.

Just as Allah ﷻ allows the non-believers to sink deeper into their disbelief and misguidance, Allah ﷻ increases the believers in guidance and righteousness.

VERSE 76

وَيَزِيدُ ٱللَّهُ ٱلَّذِينَ ٱهْتَدَوْا۟ هُدًى ۗ وَٱلْبَٰقِيَٰتُ ٱلصَّٰلِحَٰتُ خَيْرٌ عِندَ
رَبِّكَ ثَوَابًا وَخَيْرٌ مَّرَدًّا

And Allah increases in guidance those who are [rightly] guided. And the everlasting good deeds are far better with your Lord in reward and in outcome.

127 3:178 - وَلَا يَحْسَبَنَّ ٱلَّذِينَ كَفَرُوٓا۟ أَنَّمَا نُمْلِى لَهُمْ خَيْرٌ لِّأَنفُسِهِمْ ۚ إِنَّمَا نُمْلِى لَهُمْ لِيَزْدَادُوٓا۟ إِثْمًا ۚ وَلَهُمْ عَذَابٌ مُّهِينٌ

128 6:110 - وَنُقَلِّبُ أَفْـِٔدَتَهُمْ وَأَبْصَٰرَهُمْ كَمَا لَمْ يُؤْمِنُوا۟ بِهِۦٓ أَوَّلَ مَرَّةٍ وَنَذَرُهُمْ فِى طُغْيَٰنِهِمْ يَعْمَهُونَ

This is a very simple, beautiful, and profound favor of Allah ﷻ. Those who have been guided to faith, belief, and righteous deeds, Allah ﷻ increases them in guidance. He ﷻ grants them tawfīq, the ability and opportunity, to do more good along with steadfastness. "The everlasting good deeds" are mentioned in Sūrah al-Kahf as well. Allah ﷻ says, "And the everlasting good deeds are far better with your Lord in reward and hope."[129] The everlasting good deeds include every single good deed we can think of. It includes all acts of worship such as praying, fasting, giving charity, reciting Quran, supplication, and dhikr. It includes being kind to our families, our parents, children, relatives, friends, and neighbors. All of these amazing and beautiful expressions of faith are "far better with your Lord in reward and in outcome" because their consequences are everlasting. There's no comparison between the benefit of something material and the benefit of something spiritual. The benefit of wealth and power is temporary, whereas, the benefit of faith and good deeds is eternal.

In the next few verses, Allah ﷻ emphasizes these concepts by responding to the ridicule and mockery of the people of Quraysh.

VERSE 77

أَفَرَءَيْتَ ٱلَّذِى كَفَرَ بِـَٔايَـٰتِنَا وَقَالَ لَأُوتَيَنَّ مَالًا وَوَلَدًا

Have you seen the one who rejected Our verses and said, "I will surely be given wealth and children?"

129 وَالْبَاقِيَاتُ الصَّالِحَاتُ خَيْرٌ عِندَ رَبِّكَ ثَوَابًا وَخَيْرٌ أَمَلًا - 18:46

This verse was revealed in response to a certain incident that took place between one of the companions of the Prophet ﷺ, Khabbāb ibn al-Aratt, and al-ʿĀṣ ibn Wā'il, who was a non-believer. Khabbāb رضي الله عنه narrates that he was a blacksmith and had lent some money to al-ʿĀṣ ibn Wā'il. When he went to collect the loan from him al-ʿĀṣ said, "No, by Allah, I won't give it back until you reject Muḥammad ﷺ." Khabbāb replied, "Never, by Allah, I'll never reject Muḥammad ﷺ, even when you die and are resurrected." In simpler terms, he said he would never do so. al-ʿĀṣ responded, "What!? Will I be brought to life after I'm dead? If so, I'll repay you then because I'll have my wealth and children there as well."[130] This is a statement that is full of sarcasm, ridicule, mockery, derision, and arrogance. This verse was revealed in response to al-ʿĀṣ ibn Wā'il's sarcastic statement.

Look at the attitude the people of Quraysh had towards the believers. Look at their arrogance, pride, mockery, and ridicule. They were so staunch in their rejection of the truth that they mocked and ridiculed belief. That's one of the reasons why the language used in this verse has a tone of astonishment, shock, and bewilderment. It's as if the question being asked is, "Can you believe someone actually said that?" after having seen all the signs and being warned. Unfortunately, this type of attitude is very prevalent in today's society as well that is heavily influenced by materialism and all that it entails. Allah ﷻ responds to this sarcastic statement saying,

VERSE 78

أَطَّلَعَ ٱلْغَيْبَ أَمِ ٱتَّخَذَ عِندَ ٱلرَّحْمَـٰنِ عَهْدًا

Has he looked into the unseen, or has he taken a pledge

130 Bukhārī, *k. al-ijārah, b. hal yu'ājir al-rajul nafsahu min mushrik fī arḍ al-ḥarb*, 2275

from the Most Merciful?

Literally, how can he be so sure that he will have wealth and children in the Hereafter? Has he been made aware of the unseen? Does he somehow know what will happen? Or has he taken a promise from al-Raḥmān, the Most Merciful? The only way for him to be certain that he'll have wealth and family in the Hereafter is if he knows the unseen or has been promised by Allah ﷻ. What exactly is it that's making him and others like him so irrationally confident and proud? Allah ﷻ Himself answers both these questions.

VERSE 79

كَلَّا ۚ سَنَكْتُبُ مَا يَقُولُ وَنَمُدُّ لَهُۥ مِنَ ٱلْعَذَابِ مَدًّا

No! We will certainly record whatever he claims and will increase his punishment extensively.

"Kallā" in Arabic is known as the word of reprimand and scold. It literally means, "No! No way! Never!" He will not have wealth nor will he have children in the Hereafter to help him in any way, shape, or form. Rather, what he says is being recorded by the angelic scribes. His disbelief, mockery, ridicule, derision, arrogance, and pride are being recorded and will be held against him. He'll have to answer for his words and will be held accountable for them. Every single word that comes out of a person's mouth is recorded. Because of his disbelief and arrogant attitude his punishment will be extended, increased, or doubled.

VERSE 80

وَنَرِثُهُۥ مَا يَقُولُ وَيَأْتِينَا فَرْدًا

And We shall inherit from him all that he speaks of and he will come to Us all alone.

Meaning, we'll take away his wealth and family, all of his belongings and possessions, and he'll come to Us alone on the Day of Judgment. He'll be all alone on that day with no one to help or assist him. His wealth and children will be of no benefit to him whatsoever. This is an extremely profound concept and idea to reflect upon. In the life of this world, we seek help, support, and assistance through material things. We spend a lot of time, energy, and effort acquiring wealth for financial security. We invest a lot of time and energy in our children and families. However, on the Day of Judgment, if a person did not have a sound heart, if they didn't believe, then these things will be of no benefit to them. As Allah ﷻ says in Sūrah al-Shuʿarāʾ, "The Day when neither wealth nor children will be of any benefit. Only those who come before Allah with a pure heart [will be saved]."[131] The arrogant non-believer will return to Allah ﷻ alone without his wealth and family to support them. As Allah ﷻ says in Sūrah al-Anʿām, "[Today] you have come back to Us all alone as We created you the first time — leaving behind everything We have provided you with. We do not see your intercessors with you — those you claimed were Allah's partners [in worship]. All your ties have been broken and all your claims have let you down."[132]

---

131 26:88-89 - يَوْمَ لاَ يَنفَعُ مَالٌ وَلاَ بَنُونَ * إِلاَّ مَنْ أَتَى اللَّـهَ بِقَلْبٍ سَلِيمٍ

132 6:94 - وَلَقَدْ جِئْتُمُونَا فُرَادَىٰ كَمَا خَلَقْنَاكُمْ أَوَّلَ مَرَّةٍ وَتَرَكْتُم مَّا خَوَّلْنَاكُمْ وَرَاءَ ظُهُورِكُمْ وَمَا نَرَىٰ مَعَكُمْ شُفَعَاءَكُمُ الَّذِينَ زَعَمْتُمْ أَنَّهُمْ فِيكُمْ شُرَكَاءُ لَقَد تَّقَطَّعَ بَيْنَكُمْ وَضَلَّ عَنكُم مَّا كُنتُمْ تَزْعُمُونَ

LESSONS AND BENEFITS FROM VERSES 73-80

1.

Faith vs. Materialism - Throughout human history, there has been this battle between two very different value systems and ways of life; īmān and materialism. This struggle is representative of the ancient battle between belief and disbelief, truth and falsehood, good and evil. Real, true, and tangible strength and power come from the strength of a person's īmān, not their material possessions. The Prophet ﷺ said, "Truly Allah ﷻ doesn't look at your appearances or your wealth; rather, He looks at your hearts and your deeds."[133]

2.

Love of this world and its enjoyments, luxuries, comforts, and pleasures blinds one from the reality of life after death. As the Prophet ﷺ said, "Your love for something causes you to be blind and deaf."[134]

3.

A person who is unknowingly drowning in darkness continues to sink further.

4.

Allah ﷻ increases those who try their best to stay on the Straight Path in guidance.

5.

The Everlasting Good Deeds are invaluable.

---

133 Muslim, *k. al-birr wa al-ṣilah wa al-ādāb, b. taḥrīm ẓulm al-muslim wa khadhlihi wa iḥtiqārihi wa damihi wa ʿirḍihi wa mālihi,* 2654

134 Abū Dāwūd, *k. al-adab, b. fī al-hawā,* 5130

After discussing the concepts of life after death and resurrection extensively, the focus of the Sūrah now shifts to the concepts of tawḥīd and shirk (associating partners with Allah ﷻ), and the reasons why the people of Quraysh associated partners with Allah ﷻ.

VERSE 81

وَٱتَّخَذُوا۟ مِن دُونِ ٱللَّهِ ءَالِهَةً لِّيَكُونُوا۟ لَهُمْ عِزًّا

And they have taken gods other than Allah, so that they may be a source of might for them.

The Mushrikūn of Makkah, the non-believers of Quraysh, took idols and statues, stones that can't talk, inanimate objects, as deities besides Allah ﷻ. They took these stones as objects of worship, honor, strength, might, power, and support. One of the reasons why they worshipped idols was "so that they may be a source of might for them." They believed that these inanimate objects would somehow help and support them in this world and the next. They committed shirk because they thought these idols were a source of power.

VERSE 82

كَلَّا ۚ سَيَكْفُرُونَ بِعِبَادَتِهِمْ وَيَكُونُونَ عَلَيْهِمْ ضِدًّا

But no! These [gods] will deny their worship and turn against them.

Allah ﷻ again uses "kallā," the word of reprimand and rejection. No! No way! Never! There's no way possible that these idols will be able to help and support them. As a matter of fact, on the Day of Judgment, they'll be a source of punishment, regret, and remorse. These idols will turn their backs on those who worshipped them and deny that they were worshipped. The idols will be their enemies as Allah ﷻ says in Sūrah al-Naḥl, "And when the polytheists see their associate-gods, they will say, 'Our Lord! These are our associate-gods that we used to invoke besides You.' Their gods will throw a rebuttal at them, [saying,] 'You are definitely liars.'"[135] Allah ﷻ also says in Sūrah al-Baqarah, "[Consider the Day] when those who misled others will disown their followers—when they face the torment—and the bonds that united them will be cut off."[136] Here Allah ﷻ is informing them what their relationship with the idols will be like in the Hereafter. In the next

135 16:86 - وَإِذَا رَأَى الَّذِينَ أَشْرَكُوا شُرَكَاءَهُمْ قَالُوا رَبَّنَا هَٰؤُلَاءِ شُرَكَاؤُنَا الَّذِينَ كُنَّا نَدْعُو مِن دُونِكَ ۖ فَأَلْقَوْا إِلَيْهِمُ الْقَوْلَ إِنَّكُمْ لَكَاذِبُونَ

136 2:166 - إِذْ تَبَرَّأَ الَّذِينَ اتُّبِعُوا مِنَ الَّذِينَ اتَّبَعُوا وَرَأَوُا الْعَذَابَ وَتَقَطَّعَتْ بِهِمُ الْأَسْبَابُ

verse, Allah ﷻ describes their relationship with the devils in this world.

VERSE 83

أَلَمْ تَرَ أَنَّآ أَرْسَلْنَا ٱلشَّيَـٰطِينَ عَلَى ٱلْكَـٰفِرِينَ تَؤُزُّهُمْ أَزًّا

Do you [O Prophet] not see that We have sent the devils against the disbelievers, constantly inciting them?

The expression "alam tara" literally translates as "haven't you seen," but it conveys the meaning of "don't you know?" or "aren't you aware?". Aren't you aware, Prophet ﷺ, that We have surely sent the devils upon the non-believers? These devils are constantly inciting them, urging them, and pushing them towards evil, sin, and disobedience. They're constantly instigating them to disobey Allah ﷻ. The devils instigate the non-believers to persist in their disbelief and sins by showing them the short-term benefits and hiding the long-term harms.

The Prophet ﷺ was shocked, astonished, and grieved by the stubbornness, arrogance, and insistence of the Quraysh upon disbelief. How can they still disbelieve after having heard the miraculous, inimitable Quran? How can they reject me as a prophet after having seen miracles? How can they refuse to accept the truth when there are signs all around? Through this verse, Allah ﷻ provides an explanation; they've been tricked, deceived, and fooled by Satan. Allah ﷻ then consoles and comforts the Prophet ﷺ.

VERSE 84

فَلَا تَعْجَلْ عَلَيْهِمْ ۖ إِنَّمَا نَعُدُّ لَهُمْ عَدًّا

So do not be in haste against them, for indeed We are [closely] counting down their days.

"So do not be in haste against them." Meaning, don't be impatient with them. Don't ask for them to be destroyed or punished because they will be destroyed and punished anyway; either in this world or the next. There's no need for you to ask for it.

"We are [closely] counting down their days." Meaning, they only have a fixed amount of time in this world and it's coming to an end. Allah ﷻ is keeping track of their deeds and is fully aware of all of the corruption and evil they're involved with. Allah ﷻ will definitely hold them accountable for what they have done, according to His infinite wisdom and justice. Their days are numbered and every single moment of their lives is being recorded. Elsewhere, Allah ﷻ reminds the Prophet ﷺ, "Do not think [O Prophet] that Allah is unaware of what the wrongdoers do. He only delays them until a Day when [their] eyes will stare in horror—rushing forth, heads raised, never blinking, hearts void."[137] Allah ﷻ also says in Sūrah Luqmān, "We allow them enjoyment for a little while, then [in time] We will force them into a harsh torment."[138]

It's mentioned in a narration that once the ʿAbbāsid Caliph Ma'mūn al-Rashīd read Sūrah Maryam and when he came across this verse he asked ibn Simāk, one of the scholars, to say a few words regarding it. He mentioned

137 وَلَا تَحْسَبَنَّ اللَّهَ غَافِلًا عَمَّا يَعْمَلُ الظَّالِمُونَ ۚ إِنَّمَا يُؤَخِّرُهُمْ لِيَوْمٍ تَشْخَصُ فِيهِ الْأَبْصَارُ * مُهْطِعِينَ مُقْنِعِي رُءُوسِهِمْ لَا يَرْتَدُّ إِلَيْهِمْ طَرْفُهُمْ ۖ وَأَفْئِدَتُهُمْ هَوَاءٌ - 14:42-43

138 نُمَتِّعُهُمْ قَلِيلًا ثُمَّ نَضْطَرُّهُمْ إِلَىٰ عَذَابٍ غَلِيظٍ - 31:24

that when our breaths have a limited number, and that number can't be increased, then they will soon come to an end.[139] There's a famous line of poetry, "Your life is breaths that are counted, so every time you breathe, a portion of it decreases."[140] Another famous line goes, "How can you enjoy the world and its pleasures, a young man whose words and breaths are counted?"[141]

In the last few verses, Allah ﷻ spoke about some of the doubts the Mushrikūn of Makkah had regarding the concepts of tawḥīd and the ākhirah. Allah ﷻ mentioned how they were fooled and deceived by their wealth, power, and status in this world and how they sarcastically and mockingly viewed the concept of resurrection. Throughout the rest of the Sūrah, Allah ﷻ continues to discuss similar themes and concepts; namely tawḥīd and resurrection. In this next verse, Allah ﷻ explains how people will be separated and gathered into two distinct groups on the day of Judgment; 1) The Muttaqūn (God-Conscious) and 2) the Mujrimūn (Guilty). The Muttaqūn will be respected, honored, and admitted into Paradise; whereas, the Mujrimūn will be disgraced and humiliated.

VERSE 85

يَوْمَ نَحْشُرُ ٱلْمُتَّقِينَ إِلَى ٱلرَّحْمَـٰنِ وَفْدًا

On the Day We will gather the righteous before the All-Merciful as an honored delegation.

139 Qurṭubī, *al-Jāmiʿ fī Aḥkām al-Quran*, 13:512

140 Ibn Abī al-Dunyā, *Qaṣr al-Amal*, 1:132

141 ʿAbd al-Ḥaqq al-Ashbīlī, *al-ʿĀqibah fī dhikr al-mawt*, 208

In this verse, Allah ﷻ is telling us how the people of taqwā are going to be honored on the Day of Judgment. The people of taqwā are those who are mindful, conscious, and aware of Allah ﷻ, both in private and in public. Their consciousness of Allah ﷻ is the catalyst behind their attitude, character, speech, and behavior. They recognize with absolute certainty that Allah ﷻ is the All-Hearing, All-Seeing, All-Knowing, Almighty, and All-Powerful, and because of that, they are aware that whatever they say and do is being recorded. This consciousness of their deeds being recorded and one day having to answer for them drives their behavior. They try their absolute best to obey the commands of Allah ﷻ and stay away from His prohibitions. These people, the God conscious, will be gathered on the Day of Judgment as a "wafd". A "wafd" is a delegation that comes riding on horses or camels as official guests of a king or ruler. They are a group that is honored and respected as official guests.

Imagine, the people of taqwā will come as an honored delegation to the All-Merciful; they will be the official guests of Allah ﷻ, the King of all kings. The animals they'll be riding on are unique animals of the Hereafter, made out of light. ʿAlī رضي الله عنه narrated that the Messenger of Allah ﷺ said, "By the One in Whose hand is my soul, when the Muttaqūn exit their graves, they will be met by white camels that have wings with saddles of gold."[142] He then read this particular verse. ibn Kathīr رحمه الله and al-Qurṭubī رحمه الله mention another narration. "When a believer leaves his grave, he will meet the best looking form he has ever seen, and it will have the nicest fragrance. He will ask, 'Who are you?' He will reply, 'Don't you know me?' He'll say no, except that Allah ﷻ has made you sweet-smelling with a handsome face. He will say, 'I'm your good deeds, and that's how you used to beautify and apply fragrance to your deeds in the world. I rode you in the world the entire time, now ride me.'"[143] May Allah ﷻ make us among the people of taqwā. Allah ﷻ then tells us about the Mujrimūn.

142 Bayhaqī, *Shuʿab al-Īmān*, 358

143 Qurṭubī, *al-Jāmiʿ fī Aḥkām al-Quran*, 13:514

VERSE 86

وَنَسُوقُ ٱلْمُجْرِمِينَ إِلَىٰ جَهَنَّمَ وِرْدًا

And will drive the criminals to Hell in thirst.

Allah ﷻ is telling us how the non-believers, who are referred to as the Mujrimūn, are going to be humiliated and disgraced on the Day of Judgment. The word "mujrim" literally means criminal. Anyone who refuses to believe in Allah ﷻ, His Messenger ﷺ, and life after death has committed crimes in terms of belief and action. On the Day of Judgment, they will be driven and herded to Hell "wirdan," parched and thirsty. On that Day, no one will be able to speak without the permission of Allah ﷻ.

VERSE 87

لَّا يَمْلِكُونَ ٱلشَّفَـٰعَةَ إِلَّا مَنِ ٱتَّخَذَ عِندَ ٱلرَّحْمَـٰنِ عَهْدًا

None will have power to intercede, except the one who has entered into a covenant with the All-Merciful.

On the Day of Judgment, no human being will have the right to intercede on behalf of another "except those granted permission by the All-Merciful, and he will say what is correct."[144] Those who will be granted permission to intercede are the ones who have "entered into a covenant with the All-Merciful." According to several Mufassirūn (scholars qualified to interpret the Quran), the covenant is living one's life according to belief in Allah ﷻ and His Messenger ﷺ; faith and righteous deeds. ibn ʿAbbās ﵁ said, "The promise is the testimony that none has the right to be worshipped but Allah ﷻ, that the person accepts that all power and strength belong to Allah ﷻ, and he places his hope in Allah ﷻ alone."[145] ibn Masʿūd ﵁ recited this verse and said, "They have entered into a covenant with Allah ﷻ. Truly Allah ﷻ will say on the Day of Judgment, 'Whoever has a covenant with Allah should stand.' People asked, 'O Abū ʿAbd al-Raḥmān, teach us [what the covenant is].' He said, 'Say O Allah! Creator of the heavens and the earth, knower of the unseen and the seen, I certainly ask you to not allow me to do anything that will bring me close to evil and take me away from good in this world. I don't rely upon anything except Your grace, so grant me an agreement that You will fulfill on the Day of Judgment. Truly You do not break promises."[146]

ibn Masʿūd ﵁ narrates that he heard the Messenger of Allah ﷺ saying to his Companions, "Are you able to take a covenant with Allah ﷻ every morning and evening?" It was said, "O Messenger of Allah! What is that?" He said, "Every morning and evening say, 'O Allah! Creator of the heavens and the earth, knower of the unseen and the seen, truly I pledge to You in the life of this world that I bear witness that there's no being worthy of worship except for You alone without any partner, and that Muḥammad is Your slave and Messenger. Don't leave me to myself, for if you leave me to myself you will have taken me away from good and brought me close to evil. I don't rely upon anything but Your grace, so grant me an agreement that You will fulfill on the Day of Judgment. Truly You do not break promises.' When a person says that, Allah ﷻ places a seal on it and places it under His throne. On the Day of Judgment a caller will call out, 'Where are those who entered a cove-

144 لَّا يَتَكَلَّمُونَ إِلَّا مَنْ أَذِنَ لَهُ الرَّحْمَـٰنُ وَقَالَ صَوَابًا - 78:38

145 Qurṭubī, *al-Jāmiʿ fī Aḥkām al-Quran*, 13:518

146 Qurṭubī, *al-Jāmiʿ fī Aḥkām al-Quran*, 13:518

nant with Allah? They will rise and enter Paradise."[147]

Allah ﷻ now returns to the topic of those who claimed that He - may He protect us from such thoughts - has children; a particular group of Jews, Christians, and Polytheists.

VERSES 88-89

وَقَالُوا ٱتَّخَذَ ٱلرَّحْمَٰنُ وَلَدًا ﴿٨٨﴾ لَّقَدْ جِئْتُمْ شَيْـًٔا إِدًّا ﴿٨٩﴾

88 And they say, "The All-Merciful has offspring." 89 You have certainly made an outrageous claim.

During the time of the Prophet ﷺ, there were three groups of people who claimed that Allah ﷻ had offspring. A group of Jews claimed that ʿUzair was the son of Allah. Christians claimed ʿIsā ﷺ was the son of Allah, and the Polytheists claimed that the Angels were the daughters of Allah. This concept is diametrically opposed to the concept of tawḥīd; the absolute oneness of Allah ﷻ. Tawḥīd, belief in the oneness of Allah ﷻ, is the cornerstone of Islamic creed. This concept is so important that the primary purpose of all Prophets and Messengers was to explain it to their people. It is the belief that Allāh ﷻ is One without partners in His dominion, One without similitude in His essence and attributes, and One without rival in His Divinity in worship. It is the belief that Allah ﷻ alone is the Creator of the heavens and the earth and everything they contain without partner. He alone is the Nourisher, the Sustainer, the One who gives life and death, the Almighty, the All-Powerful, the All-Hearing, the All-Seeing, the All-Knowing, and the Controller of all affairs. He alone has the right to be worshipped

147 Zaylaʿī, *Takhrīj al-Kashshāf*, 2:339

and He is completely unique. Nothing in this universe resembles Him in any way, shape, or form.

Claiming that Allah ﷻ has offspring is absolutely outrageous, atrocious, and unbelievable. How could someone have the audacity to say such a thing? This statement is so outrageous, that Allah ﷻ Himself says, "You have certainly made an outrageous claim." Allah ﷻ describes how atrocious this claim is when He says,

VERSES 90-92

تَكَادُ ٱلسَّمَٰوَٰتُ يَتَفَطَّرۡنَ مِنۡهُ وَتَنشَقُّ ٱلۡأَرۡضُ وَتَخِرُّ ٱلۡجِبَالُ هَدًّا
﴿٩٠﴾ أَن دَعَوۡاْ لِلرَّحۡمَٰنِ وَلَدٗا ﴿٩١﴾ وَمَا يَنۢبَغِي لِلرَّحۡمَٰنِ أَن يَتَّخِذَ وَلَدًا

90 It almost causes the heavens to be torn apart, the earth to split asunder, the mountains to crumble to pieces, 91 that they attribute offspring to the All-Merciful. 92 It does not befit the Lord of Mercy to have offspring.

When they make this atrocious and outrageous claim of Allah ﷻ having a child, it upsets and angers the entire creation of Allah ﷻ. When the heavens heard this they were about to rupture and burst apart, the earth was on the verge of splitting, and the mountains would crumble and collapse turning to dust. They are offended, angered, and enraged because they are the creations of Allah ﷻ, built upon the foundation of tawḥīd. All created things in this universe are in total and complete submission to Allah ﷻ, except those among mankind and jinn who refuse to do so. ibn ʿAbbās said, "The heavens, earth, mountains and all of creation are terrified and alarmed by shirk, except for mankind and jinn."[148]

The reason why these creations were enraged is because "they attribute offspring to the All-Merciful. It does not befit the Lord of Mercy to have offspring." These magnificent creations of Allah ﷻ were enraged, angered, and alarmed that people attributed offspring to the All-Merciful because of their respect, recognition, and honor of Allah ﷻ. It's not appropriate or befitting for the All-Merciful, the Almighty, the All-Powerful, the Self-Sufficient to have offspring. He's free and above the need to have children. There's nothing similar to Him in any way, shape, or form. He ﷻ is not in need of anything, whereas, everything and everyone is in need of Him ﷻ.

In a ḥadīth qudsī, Allah ﷻ says, "The son of Adam denied Me and he had no right to do so. And the son of Adam reviled Me and he had no right to do so. As for his denying Me, it is his saying that I will not resurrect him as I created him in the beginning, but resurrecting him is not more difficult for Me than creating him in the first place. And as for his reviling Me, it is his saying that Allah has taken a son, but I am Allah, the One, the Self-Sufficient Master, I beget not nor was I begotten, and there is none co-equal or comparable unto Me."[149]

VERSE 93

إِن كُلُّ مَن فِي ٱلسَّمَٰوَٰتِ وَٱلْأَرْضِ إِلَّآ ءَاتِي ٱلرَّحْمَٰنِ عَبْدًا

There is no one in the heavens and the earth except that they will come to the All-Merciful as a slave.

148 Al-Ṭabarī, *Jāmiʿ al-Bayān*, 18:258

149 Bukhārī, *k. al-tafsīr*, 4974

Every single thing that has existed, that exists, and that will exist in the heavens and the earth - angels, humans, and jinn - will come to Allah ﷻ, the All-Merciful, on the Day of Judgment as a slave and servant. This is a very powerful and profound concept to reflect upon. In the life of this world, people may take pride and find value in their lineage, wealth, properties, power, and authority. However, on the Day of Judgment, every single person will be a slave standing before Allah ﷻ, awaiting judgment.

VERSES 94-95

لَّقَدْ أَحْصَىٰهُمْ وَعَدَّهُمْ عَدًّا ﴿٩٤﴾ وَكُلُّهُمْ ءَاتِيهِ يَوْمَ ٱلْقِيَـٰمَةِ فَرْدًا ﴿٩٥﴾

94 Indeed, He fully knows them and has counted them precisely. 95 And each of them will return to Him on the Day of Judgment all alone.

Allah's ﷻ knowledge is infinite and limitless; it is beyond human comprehension, without beginning or end. He ﷻ knows everything that has happened, that is happening, and that will happen. He ﷻ knew the exact number of His creation before He brought them into existence; He's precisely counted how many individuals there will be, from the beginning of time until the end of time, and their varying conditions. Allah ﷻ is highlighting that every single human being is under His control, sovereignty, command, and planning. Every single thing has been determined.

On that Day, every single person will come to Allah ﷻ alone without anyone or anything to help them. They will have no wealth, property, title, power, influence, or children to aid and assist them. They will have no one and nothing to help them and turn to except for Allah ﷻ. As Allah ﷻ says in Sūrah al-Shuʿārāʾ, "The Day when there will not benefit [anyone] wealth or children. But only one who comes to Allah with a sound heart."[150] Through this verse, Allah ﷻ is making us realize who we truly are as human beings and the nature of our relationship with him; we are simply His slaves and He's our Master. On that day, Allah ﷻ will judge as He wills and He is the Most Just who doesn't oppress people in any way whatsoever.

LESSONS AND BENEFITS FROM VERSES 81-95

1.

The absurdity and gravity of associating partners with Allah ﷻ

2.

The people of taqwā will be honored on the Day of Judgment.

3.

Intercession will be granted and accepted from the righteous on the Day of Judgment.

4.

The reality of our relationship with Allah ﷻ; He is our Creator, Lord, and Master, and we are simply His slaves and servants.

150 يَوْمَ لَا يَنفَعُ مَالٌ وَلَا بَنُونَ * إِلَّا مَنْ أَتَى اللَّهَ بِقَلْبٍ سَلِيمٍ - 26:88-89

The main objective of the last passage is to firmly establish the concept of tawḥīd and pure servitude to Allah ﷻ. In the last passage of the Sūrah, Allah ﷻ addresses three topics:

1.

The believers and how they're loved by Allah ﷻ and all of His creation

2.

The Quran has been made simple and easy to understand upon the tongue of the Prophet ﷺ. The language of the verses is straightforward and easy to understand so that whoever listens to it with an open heart and mind, will understand the concepts of tawḥīd, prophethood, resurrection, morals, values, ethics, principles, and general guidance.

3.

A severe warning of destruction to the people of Quraysh, just like those nations and communities that came before them. If they realize that this world has to come to an end, and they recognize the gravity of death, they will fear it and fear its consequences.

VERSE 96

إِنَّ ٱلَّذِينَ ءَامَنُوا۟ وَعَمِلُوا۟ ٱلصَّـٰلِحَـٰتِ سَيَجْعَلُ لَهُمُ ٱلرَّحْمَـٰنُ وُدًّا

Indeed, those who have believed and done righteous deeds - the Most Merciful will appoint for them affection.

In this verse, Allah ﷻ is telling us about one of the most beautiful, yet subtle, consequences and rewards of īmān. Those who truly believe in Allah ﷻ, the Prophet ﷺ, and life after death, and that īmān translates into all types of righteous deeds - those that are obligatory, recommended, and voluntary - then Allah ﷻ plants love and affection for them in the hearts of others. People around them will be naturally drawn towards them and the light of īmān in their hearts. Not only will the people around them be drawn towards them, but the Angels in the heavens will love them as well. Allah ﷻ creates an environment of mutual love, affection, care, and goodwill around them. This reward is for those whose faith is firmly rooted in their hearts, resulting in the light of that faith emanating through their speech and behavior.

Abū Hurayrah رضي الله عنه narrated that the Prophet ﷺ said, "Verily, whenever Allah loves a servant of His, He calls Jibrīl and says, 'O Jibrīl, verily I love so-and-so, so love him.' Thus, Jibrīl will love him. Then, he (Jibrīl) will call out to the dwellers of the heavens, 'Verily, Allah loves so-and-so, so you too must love him.' Then the dwellers of the heavens love him and he will be given acceptance on the earth. Whenever Allah hates a servant of His, He calls Jibrīl and says, 'O Jibrīl, verily I hate so-and-so, so hate him.' Thus, Jibrīl will hate him. Then, he (Jibrīl) will call out amongst the dwellers of the heavens, 'Verily, Allah hates so-and-so, so you too must hate him.' Then, the dwellers of the heavens hate him and hatred for him will be placed on the earth."[151] This phenomenon is something that we can experience, feel, and see with our own eyes. When a person devotes their entire being, their entire life to Allah ﷻ and His dīn, He ﷻ fills the hearts of believers with love for him. Harim ibn Ḥayyān used to say, "No one turns their hearts towards Allah ﷻ except that Allah ﷻ turns the hearts of the believers towards them, granting them their love and grace."[152] Allah ﷻ then explains that the Quran has been made easy to understand.

VERSE 97

فَإِنَّمَا يَسَّرْنَـٰهُ بِلِسَانِكَ لِتُبَشِّرَ بِهِ ٱلْمُتَّقِينَ وَتُنذِرَ بِهِۦ قَوْمًا لُّدًّا

Indeed, We have made this [Quran] easy in your own language [O Prophet] so with it you may give good news to the righteous and warn those who are stubborn.

Meaning, Allah ﷻ has facilitated both learning and understanding the Quran. It's easy to read, memorize, listen to, study, understand, and act upon. As Allah ﷻ says in Sūrah al-Qamar, "And We have certainly made the Quran easy to remember. So is there anyone who will be mindful?"[153] All of these things have been further facilitated through your language, the language of Arabic. Allah ﷻ has revealed the Quran in the pure, eloquent, emotive, beautiful, and powerful language of Arabic.

151 Muslim, *k. al-birr wa al-ṣilah wa al-ādāb, b. idhā aḥabba Allah ʿabd ḥabbabahu ilā ʿibādihi,* 2637

152 Qurṭubī, *al-Jāmiʿ fī Aḥkām al-Quran*, 13:527

153 وَلَقَدْ يَسَّرْنَا الْقُرْآنَ لِلذِّكْرِ فَهَلْ مِن مُّدَّكِرٍ - 54:17

One of the reasons for facilitating the Quran is so that the Prophet ﷺ could give good news to the people of taqwā and warn the people who are "ludd," stubborn. Through the Quran, the Prophet ﷺ gives the people of taqwā the good news of forgiveness, pardon, grace, mercy, reward, and Paradise. At the same time, he warns the non-believers, those who are described as being stubborn, about the anger, wrath, and punishment of Allah ﷻ. "Ludd" refers to people who have deviated away from the truth and are inclined towards falsehood. Allah ﷻ then concludes the Sūrah with an extremely powerful reminder saying,

VERSE 98

وَكَمْ أَهْلَكْنَا قَبْلَهُم مِّن قَرْنٍ هَلْ تُحِسُّ مِنْهُم مِّنْ أَحَدٍ أَوْ
تَسْمَعُ لَهُمْ رِكْزًا

How many generations We have destroyed before them! Do you perceive a single one of them now, or hear as much as a whisper?

This verse is in the form of a rhetorical question. Rhetorical questions are used to emphasize a particular point or to stress the importance of something. The question is posed not to elicit a specific answer, but rather to encourage the listener to consider a message or viewpoint.

Allah ﷻ is reminding the non-believers of Makkah about how many generations and communities of the past have been destroyed because of their rejection of the signs of Allah ﷻ and rejection of messengers. They no longer exist; they have been completely wiped off the face of this earth. There have been many kings and rulers who ruled over vast empires, had unlimited power, wealth and authority, lived in extreme luxury, but when the punishment of Allah ﷻ came to them because of their disbelief and sins, they were destroyed in such a way that not even a sound or whisper is heard of them; they're completely gone without a trace.

This brings us to the end of this very noble, beautiful, gentle, and eloquent Sūrah. One of the most common themes throughout the entire Sūrah is raḥmah, the infinite, limitless, and divine mercy of Allah ﷻ. The divine mercy of Allah ﷻ is something that is absolutely unique and amazing. As human beings all of us experience and express varying degrees and levels of mercy in different ways. For example, all acts of kindness, sympathy, generosity, care, concern, and love are expressions of mercy. But our expressions and experiences of mercy are finite and limited; whereas, the mercy of Allah ﷻ is infinite and limitless. As Allah ﷻ Himself tells us, "And my mercy encompasses every single thing."[154]

Imām al-Ālūsī ؒ comments that the nature of the Divine Mercy is that it "is vast, it reaches all things... there isn't any Muslim nor disbeliever, nor obedient or disobedient who is not being constantly overturned in this world by [His] generous bounty."[155] May Allah ﷻ continue to shower us with His divine mercy!

---

154 وَرَحْمَتِي وَسِعَتْ كُلَّ شَيْءٍ - 7:156

155 Ālūsī, *Rūḥ al-Maʿānī*,

APPENDIX

STRUCTURE AND COHESION OF SŪRAH MARYAM

MUNIR ELTAL

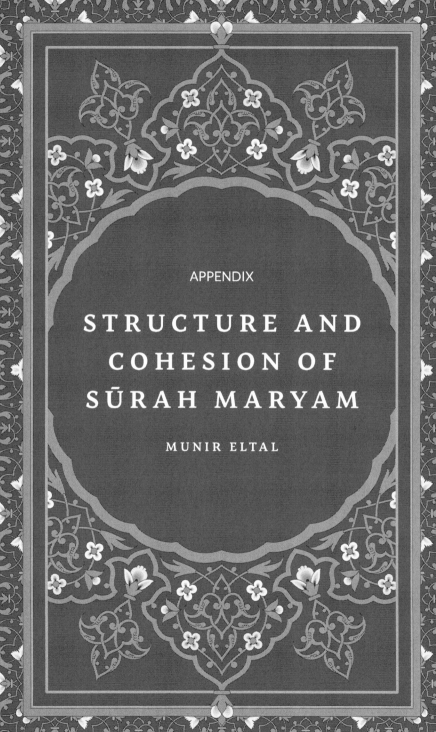

In the Name of Allah, the Most Merciful, the Very Merciful. All thanks and praise are due to Allah ﷻ, the Master of all creation, and may His blessings be upon His last and final Messenger, Muḥammad ﷺ, his family, his companions, and those who follow them until the end of times.

As has been explained by the author, every verse of Sūrah Maryam contains rich meanings that one can learn and apply to their life. Another aspect of the Sūrah, which is not as well-known, is how the Sūrah is organized. How do the verses come together to form a coherent whole, whose placement of verses contributes to a well-organized and methodological message? And how might that structuring lend itself to deeper meanings not as apparent on an initial read-through?

Before one answers these questions, it is important to ask why this study is meaningful in the first place. Why should one study how Allah ﷻ organized the placement of His verses? There are four of reasons worth discussing:

1.

Allah ﷻ is the Best of Speakers and His Speech is the Best of All Speech - Allah ﷻ says in the beginning of Sūrah ar-Raḥmān, "The Most Merciful, He taught the Quran, created man, [and] taught him al-bayān."[1] Bayān involves both expressing oneself and understanding what has been expressed by others. It can be defined as eloquence, clear speech, explaining, the ability to

1 الرَّحْمَـٰنُ * عَلَّمَ الْقُرْآنَ * خَلَقَ الْإِنسَانَ * عَلَّمَهُ الْبَيَانَ - 55:1-4

express oneself, or elucidating.

Allah ﷻ taught humans how to speak and part of communicating effectively is having organized speech. If all coherent speech is clearly organized, what can be said of the speech of the Teacher of all speech? Part of the agreed upon definition of the Quran is that it is the inimitable speech of Allah ﷻ. Nothing can, or will, ever come close to His words in all praiseworthy manners. Allah ﷻ Himself calls the Quran "bayān," so one should take note of how He organized His perfect words.

Additionally, in Sūrah al-Kahf, Allah ﷻ says, "Say, 'If the sea were ink for [writing] the words of my Lord, the sea would be exhausted before the words of my Lord were exhausted, even if We brought the like of it as a supplement.'"[2] And He ﷻ also says in Sūrah Luqmān, "And if whatever trees upon the earth were pens and the sea [was ink], replenished thereafter by seven [more] seas, the words of Allah would not be exhausted. Indeed, Allah is Exalted in Might and Wise."[3] These verses point to Allah's ability to articulate meanings with many layers of understanding. The more one delves into His verses, the more one benefits and finds. How He structured His words may be another layer on top of the already innumerable methods of accessing Allah's words.

2.

All of Creation is Organized[4] – Humans are encouraged by Allah ﷻ in a number of verses to contemplate the harmony of His creation. In Sūrah al-Wāqi'ah, Allah ﷻ says, "I swear by the positions of the stars–A mighty oath, if you only knew–that this is truly a noble Quran."[5] Allah ﷻ tied the precision of the star's positions to the Quran. If the heavens, the earth, the cells in our bodies and even the atoms forming those objects are organized, then how can the speech of Allah ﷻ not be?

Science and mathematics are essentially the study of how Allah ﷻ orga-

---

2 قُل لَّوْ كَانَ الْبَحْرُ مِدَادًا لِّكَلِمَاتِ رَبِّي لَنَفِدَ الْبَحْرُ قَبْلَ أَن تَنفَدَ كَلِمَاتُ رَبِّي وَلَوْ جِئْنَا بِمِثْلِهِ مَدَدًا -18:109

3 وَلَوْ أَنَّمَا فِي الْأَرْضِ مِن شَجَرَةٍ أَقْلَامٌ وَالْبَحْرُ يَمُدُّهُ مِن بَعْدِهِ سَبْعَةُ أَبْحُرٍ مَّا نَفِدَتْ كَلِمَاتُ اللَّهِ إِنَّ اللَّهَ عَزِيزٌ حَكِيمٌ - 31:27

4 This point is argued in more detail by Shaykh Abdu l-Hamīd al-Farāhī in his book, Dalāil an-Nidhām

5 فَلَا أُقْسِمُ بِمَوَاقِعِ النُّجُومِ * وَإِنَّهُ لَقَسَمٌ لَّوْ تَعْلَمُونَ عَظِيمٌ * إِنَّهُ لَقُرْآنٌ كَرِيمٌ - 56:75

nized His creation. If not for the regular patterns one witnesses in the world, documenting observations into comprehensible textbooks and research papers would be near-impossible. Just as creation has a structure one can follow, the structure of Allah's speech is just as observable.

3.

There Are Claims That the Quran is Unorganized - There are many documented cases of non-Muslims critiquing the Quran for what they perceive to be a lack of cohesion. The famous French philosopher, Voltaire, wrote scathingly about Islam. On the Quran, in particular, he is recorded to have stated, "The Qur'an is a rhapsody without liaison, without order, without art; it is said nevertheless that this boring book is a very beautiful book—I am referring here to the Arabs, who pretend it is written with an elegance and a purity that no one has approached since." [6]

There are also those such as Thomas Carlyle, who generally spoke favorably about Islam. He said in praise of the Messenger ﷺ, "It is a great shame for anyone to listen to the accusation that Islam is a lie and that Muhammad was a fabricator and a deceiver. We saw that he remained steadfast upon his principles, with firm determination; kind and generous, compassionate, pious, virtuous, with real manhood, hardworking and sincere. Besides all these qualities, he was lenient with others, tolerant, kind, cheerful and praiseworthy and perhaps he would joke and tease his companions. He was just, truthful, smart, pure, magnanimous and present-minded; his face was radiant as if he had lights within him to illuminate the darkest of nights; he was a great man by nature who was not educated in a school nor nurtured by a teacher as he was not in need of any of this."[7] Which makes his criticism of the Quran all the more impactful when he said, "I must say, it is as toilsome reading as I ever undertook. A wearisome confused jumble, crude, incondite; endless iterations, long-windedness, entanglement [...] insupportable stupidity in short!"[8]

Then there are the Muslims, though sincere in their questioning, who

---

6 Voltaire, "Alcoran" in Dictionnaire de philosophie, cited in Michel Cuypers and Geneviève Gobillot, Le Coran (Paris: Le Cavalier Bleu, 2007)

7 Carlyle, Thomas Carlyle, On Heroes, Hero Worship and the Heroic in History, ed. Archibald MacMechan (Boston: Athenaeum, 1901)

8 Ibid.

are confused about how Allah ﷻ organized His speech. What many fail to realize is that the Quran has its own standard of structure, one which is better than anything on offer from Allah's creation. Despite the lofty standards, Allah ﷻ tells us in the beginning of Sūrah Yūsūf, "No doubt We sent it down as an Arabic Quran so that you all may understand [it]."[9] The coherence of the Quran is accessible, and this study will demonstrate, at a surface level, how well-structured this Sūrah is.

4.

It is a Potential Source for Interpreting the Quran - Tafsīr (Explanation) of the Quran with the Quran is one of the main sources for unlocking the Quran's meanings. Imām al-Suyūṭī ﵀ summarized this methodology saying, "The scholars have said: Whoever wishes to interpret the Quran, he should first turn to the Quran itself. This is because what has been narrated briefly in one place might be explained in detail in another place, and what is summarized in one place might be explained in another."[10] In simpler terms, using the surrounding context can help to elucidate the meaning of Allah's words. By understanding how Allah ﷻ organized the verses, qualified scholars may be able to uncover an additional layer of context by which to interpret a sūrah.

ORGANIZING TOOLS

Before beginning the breakdown of the structure of Sūrah Maryam, it is important to understand the different methods of organizing communication. The study of the composition of a sūrah involves several aspects. It has been observed that Allah ﷻ utilizes the following tools to varying degrees, with each providing a unique benefit.

Linear Coherence

The first aspect is called linear coherence, which concerns the linear flow, continuity or sequential arrangement of the Quran. In what way is one

9 إِنَّا أَنزَلْنَاهُ قُرْآنًا عَرَبِيًّا لَّعَلَّكُمْ تَعْقِلُونَ - 12:2

10 al-Suyūṭī, Al-Itqān fī 'ulūm al-Qurān

verse or topic connected to the next? Linear coherence has the most written about it with regards to the Quran, and the author sufficiently explained the transition of one verse to the next as has been shown above, so there will not be too much focus on this method.

Parallelism

There are two main types of symmetrical patterns. The first we will explore is called Parallelism. This is when parts of a composition are ordered on the pattern of ABC/A'B'C'. For example, Allah ﷻ says in Sūrah Qāf (transliteration provided where needed)[11]:

A - But they **denied**
B - the **truth (al-haqq)** when it came to them,
C - so they are in a **confused** condition. (5)
D - Have they not looked at the heaven above them - **how We structured it** and **adorned it** and [how] it has no rifts? (6) And the earth - **We spread it out** and **cast therein** firmly set mountains and **made grow** therein [something] of every beautiful kind, (7) Giving insight and a reminder for every servant who turns [to Allah]. (8) And We have sent down blessed rain from the sky and **made grow** thereby gardens and grain from the harvest (9) And lofty palm trees having fruit arranged in layers - (10) As provision for the servants, and We have **given life thereby to a dead land**. Thus, is the **resurrection**. (11)
A' - The people of Noah **denied** before them, and the companions of the well and Thamud (12) And 'Aad and Pharaoh and the brothers of Lot (13) And the companions of the thicket and the people of Tubba'. All **denied** the messengers,
B' - so My threat was **justly fulfilled (haqqa).** (14)
C' - Did We fail in the first creation? But they are in **confusion**
D' - over a **new creation**. (15)

Each item corresponds to its source in the list. The point is that the parallel terms must have some conspicuous relationship, whether it is a relationship of similarity, opposites, or something else.

Parallelism is an extremely common device in poetics and rhetoric, because it is simple, intuitive, aesthetically appealing, and poetically moving.[12] In terms of the Quran, if one finds a parallel pattern, then Allah ﷻ could be drawing attention to an otherwise overlooked relationship between two

11 Heavenly Order. "Sūrah Qāf (Part 2)." 2 Oct. 2020, https://heavenlyorder.substack.com/p/surah-qaaf-part-2

12 Ali Khan, Nouman and Sharif Randhawa. Divine Speech: Exploring the Quran as Literature. Bayyinah Institute, 2016.

items. Conversely, where all but one item corresponds in a parallel structure, it may be that Allah ﷻ is teaching us a lesson about the subtle differences.

Mirror Composition

The second type of symmetrical form may be called inverted parallelism, or mirror composition: it is where the terms or ideas are presented in one order but then repeated in the reverse order. This follows the pattern AB-C/C'B'A'. In a similar vein, the term ring composition is used to describe such a structure when it contains a discrete center. It could either have a stand-alone centerpiece that connects the two halves (as in ABCB'A') or simply be a mirror composition on a large or complex scale, such as ABCD/D'C'B'A', in which D/D' might be considered the center. For example, the story of Mūsā ؑ in Sūrah al-Qaṣaṣ appears to be structured in this manner[13]:

A – Prologue (1-6)
B – Mūsā is thrown in the water and lives (7-8)
C – Fir'awn's wife asks him for a favor (9)
D – The sister of Mūsā is sent to Fir'awn and her speech is accepted (10-12)
E – Mūsā is returned to his mother (13)
F – Mūsā unsuccessfully tries to help two men (14-22)
F' – Mūsā successfully helps two women (23-24)
E' – Mūsā meets his father-in-law (25-28)
D' – Mūsā is sent to Fir'awn and his speech is rejected
C' - Fir'awn asks Hāmān for a favor (38)
B' - Fir'awn and his army are drowned (39-42)
A' – Epilogue (43-52)

Several features are significant about ring composition. First, it may occur on different scales. It can be seen in sentences, passages, or even an entire book. In some cases, as is common in the Quran, a large-scale ring composition consists, in turn, of smaller rings.

Finally, understanding ring structure is important for understanding the meaning of a composition. In a ring composition, usually "the meaning is located in the middle;"[14] that is, the center of the composition literally un-

13 Heavenly Order. "Sūrah Al-Qaṣaṣ (Part 1)." 6 Nov. 2020, heavenlyorder.substack.com/p/surah-al-qaa-part-1

14 See Mary Douglas, Thinking in Circles: An Essay on Ring Composition (New Haven/London: Yale University Press, 2007)

derscores the central idea. The two halves of the composition may be seen as elaborations of that theme, and the beginning and the ending segments (A and A') introduce and conclude that theme. Moreover, the ring structure points to common themes that underlie the two corresponding terms or segments on the opposite sides of the structure. In essence the ring manifests the relationship between the parts and reveals the logic of the composition. It is important to add that the relationship between the two corresponding segments (e.g., B and B') does not always have to be immediately obvious. The discovery of a ring structure forces the audience to contemplate and uncover the relationship between the corresponding parts. [15]

Integrative Coherence

The fourth aspect of coherence to explore is called the integrative coherence of a sūrah. This is concerned with how different verses, passages, or sections within a sūrah, or even between separate sūrahs, are interconnected by key terms, verbal roots, images, parallel expressions, or even sound patterns that they share. To simplify, we will call these unifying items anchors.

Although this sort of study is already known more formally as intertextuality, we will use the term "integrative coherence" to emphasize the role of these anchors in:

- Integrating different parts of a section together;
- Linking separate sections of a sūrah, thereby helping to unify it; and
- Linking verses or passages from separate sūrahs[16]

Holistic Coherence

Finally, each of these approaches contributes to understanding the sūrah's holistic coherence; how the sūrah is united into a consistent and distinct whole. In this regard, one might be interested in identifying a motif, an overarching idea that unites and explains all of the sūrah's contents or components. In addition to seeing the unity of an individual sūrah and how each part of it fits into the scheme of the whole, one might also be interested in understanding the role of the sūrah in a broader surah pair or group, or in

15 Ibid.

16 Ali Khan, Nouman and Sharif Randhawa. Divine Speech: Exploring the Quran as Literature. Bayyinah Institute, 2016.

the Quran as a whole.[17]

The study of holistic coherence is a method of the reader inquiring, "Why is this verse placed in this Sūrah and not another one?" The immediate context creates a meaning that may be altered if the verse were placed elsewhere in the Quran.

Final Notes

It is important to state that multiple organizational tools may be used to explore a single sūrah, and each tool may yield meanings different, but not contrary, to the others. As we will observe, the same passage may contain multiple structures layered on top of one-another.

How we split up the passages and verses may also seem strange at first, as not every structure is split perfectly at the end of a verse. It is possible that one structure ends halfway through a verse and another begins at the second half. It may also be the case that one section references a short phrase, while the corresponding section is an entire paragraph. These choices will all be justified below, but consider that Allah's standards for organizing His words may not match with what we consider "normal" from our limited experiences. What is explained briefly in one part may be expounded in a linked set of verses elsewhere.

Please keep in mind that the outlined observations below are just that; observations. We make no claims as to having presented the structure of a given verse or section, let alone the entire Sūrah. It is very possible that others will disagree with our proposed demarcations and that there are arguably better ways of splitting this Sūrah up. As this is not meant to be an exhaustive study of Sūrah Maryam's structure, alternative plausible structures will be omitted for brevity.

We have also tried our best to avoid making conclusions about the text based on a presented structure. In other words, this appendix is not meant to be a tafsīr of the Quran's meanings. The hope is that qualified scholars take this work and use it appropriately.

With the above terminology understood, one may now begin the study of the structure of Sūrah Maryam. We will be omitting any Arabic from the forthcoming analysis and only providing transliterations when needed to draw a connection. Consult the original Arabic - provided in the main text

17 Ibid.

by the author above - for the original wording of the Quran for any verses referenced below.

Big Picture

Because of the length and complexity of Sūrah Maryam, we will begin with a macroscopic view of the contents and then slowly work our way down to the microscopic level.

Overall, the Sūrah appears to be organized in a ring composition as shown below, with verse numbers given in parenthesis:

A – Divine Intervention at Birth (2-40)
B – Ibrāhīm and His Father (41-50)
C' – Our Forefathers in Faith (51-58)
B' – Path to Salvation (59-65)
A' – Denying the True Reality (66-98)

Note the omission of the first verse. We will come back to it towards the conclusion of this section.

As for the overall structure, we will return to the connection between each of these sections once we've analyzed them in detail below.

Section [A] - Divine Intervention at Birth

The beginning section of Sūrah Maryam focuses on the stories of Zakariyyā ﷺ and Maryam ﷺ. When observed more closely, it appears that the section can be split into four smaller parts, each focusing on a different narrative.

The first half of Section [A] contains two rings. The first ring is about Zakariyyā ﷺ and the second ring is about Yaḥyā ﷺ. The ring corresponding to Zakariyyā ﷺ looks as so:

A1 - [This is] a mention of the mercy of your Lord to His servant Zakariyyā (2)

  A2 - When he called to his Lord a private supplication. (3)

    A3 - He said, "My Lord, indeed my bones have weakened, and my head has filled with white, and never have I been in my supplication to You, my Lord, unhappy. (4) And indeed, I fear the successors after me, and my wife has been barren,

      A4 - so give me from Yourself an heir (5) Who will inherit me and inherit from the family of Jacob.

        A5 - And make him, my Lord, pleasing [to You]." (6)

      A4' - [He was told], "O Zakariyyā, indeed We give you good news of a boy whose name will be Yaḥyā. We have not assigned to any before [this] name." (7)

    A3' - He said, "My Lord, how will I have a boy when my wife has been barren and I have reached extreme old age?" (8) [An angel] said, "Thus [it will be]; your Lord says, 'It is easy for Me, for I created you before, while you were nothing.' " (9)

  A2' - [Zakariyyā] said, "My Lord, make for me a sign." He said, "Your sign is that you will not speak to the people for three nights, [being] sound." (10)

A1' - So he came out to his people from the prayer chamber and signaled to them to exalt [Allah] in the morning and afternoon. (11)

Connections

- [A1/A1'] - Allah's mentioning (dhikr) of His servant, Zakariyyā ﷺ, is paired with the mentioning and praising of Allah ﷻ (sabbiḥū) by His servants.
- [A2/A2'] - Zakariyyā ﷺ begins the Sūrah calling to Allah ﷻ quietly so that no one else would hear, and ends the Section being only able to speak to Allah ﷻ with no one else capable of hearing him, even if he desired so.
- [A3/A3'] - At first Zakariyyā ﷺ explains that his old age and barren ('āqirā) wife's condition mean that they cannot have children through their own means, and then he repeats these traits, old and barren ('āqirā), after being shocked with the good news of a son.
- [A4/A4'] - Zakariyyā ﷺ prays for an heir that will inherit from him and is then given the good news of one. Interestingly, Zakariyyā ﷺ is told that his son will have a unique name, i.e., one that he inherited from no one before him.
- [A5] - This section can be argued to center on the trait of being pleasing to Allah ﷻ (raḍiyā). As we will see in the forthcoming sections, the motif of having a good family runs throughout this Sūrah, which will continue to highlight the importance of praying for righteous children who are pleasing to Allah ﷻ.

The ring for Yaḥyā ﷺ appears to be structured as follows:

A6 - [Allah] said, "O Yaḥyā, take the Scripture with determination." And We gave him wisdom [while yet] a boy (12)
A7 - And affection from Us and purity,
A8 - and he was fearing of Allah (13)
A7' - And dutiful to his parents, and he was not a disobedient tyrant. (14)
A6' - And safety and protection are upon him the day he was born and the day he dies and the day he is raised alive. (15)

Connections

- [A6/A6'] - The ring begins by informing us of Yaḥyā ﷺ when he was still a child; i.e., the beginning of life. The corresponding verse grants us the remaining details of his life span as it tells us how he will die and be resurrected. His entire life was thus summarized in these paired verses.
- [A7/A7'] - Both parts give two praiseworthy attributes of Yaḥyā ﷺ.
- [A8] - The fifth description of Yaḥyā ﷺ, which sits in the middle of the entire ring, is Yaḥyā's quality of being conscious of Allah ﷻ (taqiyyā). Connecting back to the ring that focused on Zakariyyā ﷺ, it may be that the hallmark of a child that is pleasing to Allah ﷻ (raḍiyyā) is one who is always conscious of Allah ﷻ (taqiyyā).

The second half of Section [A] teaches us about Maryam ﷺ and her child, ʿĪsā ﷺ. This half can also be split into two parts, with each part forming its own parallel structure. The first parallel structure covers the story of Maryam ﷺ all the way through 'Īsā's sermon:

Intro: And mention in the Book ⌜O Prophet, the story of⌝ Maryam

A9 - when she withdrew from her family to a place in the east, (16)

> **A10** - screening herself off from them.
>
> > **A11** - Then We sent to her Our angel, appearing before her as a man, perfectly formed. (17) She appealed, "I truly seek refuge in the Most Compassionate from you! ⌜So leave me alone⌝ if you are God-fearing." (18) He responded, "I am only a messenger from your Lord, ⌜sent⌝ to bless you with a pure son." (19)
> >
> > > **A12** - She wondered, "How can I have a son when no man has ever touched me, nor am I unchaste?" (20)
> > >
> > > > **A13** - He replied, "So will it be! Your Lord says, 'It is easy for Me. And We will make him a sign for humanity and a mercy from Us.' It is a matter ⌜already⌝ decreed." (21)

A9' - So she conceived him and withdrew with him to a remote place. (22)

> **A10'** - Then the pains of labor drove her to the trunk of a palm tree. She cried, "Alas! I wish I had died before this, and was a thing long forgotten!" (23)
>
> > **A11'** - So a voice reassured her from below her, "Do not grieve! Your Lord has provided a stream at your feet. (24) And shake the trunk of this palm tree towards you, it will drop fresh, ripe dates upon you. (25) So, eat and drink, and put your heart at ease
> >
> > > **A12'** - But if you see any of the people, say, 'I have vowed silence to the Most Compassionate, so I am not talking to anyone today.'" (26) Then she returned to her people, carrying him. They said ⌜in shock⌝, "O Maryam! You have certainly done a horrible thing! (27) O sister of Hārūn! Your father was not an indecent man, nor was your mother unchaste." (28) So, she pointed to the baby. They exclaimed, "How can we talk to someone who is an infant in the cradle?" (29)
> > >
> > > > **A13'** - ⌜'Īsā⌝ declared, "I am truly a servant of Allah. He has destined me to be given the Scripture and to be a prophet. (30) He has made me a blessing wherever I go, and bid me to establish prayer and give alms-tax as long as I live, (31) and to be kind to my mother. He has not made me arrogant or defiant. (32) Safety and protection are with me the day I was born, the day I die, and the day I will be raised back to life!" (33) That is 'Īsā, the son of Maryam –

Connections

- [A9/A9'] - The structure begins by mentioning Maryam عليها السلام as she withdrew (intabadhat) from her family to worship. The corresponding verse also tells of her withdrawing (intabadhat), but this time with a child in her womb, drawing a possible connection between pregnancy and a recommendation to increase in worship.
- [A10/A10'] - Maryam عليها السلام screening herself from people is paired with her labor and delivery. While there is the obvious connection of a woman being in private as she gives birth, there is also the contrast between her attempt to be physically forgotten when she withdrew for worship and her wish to be mentally forgotten during childbirth.
- [A11/A11'] - Both parts have a messenger from Allah ﷻ being sent to Maryam عليها السلام to give her good news and provide her with provisions.

She's given a child and food and drink. Interestingly, the verses in [A11'] include "and put your heart at ease" (waqarrī 'aynā) which is similar to the wording of the prayer we are encouraged to say when asking for righteous children, "And those who say, 'Our Master, gift us from our spouses and children those who put our heart at ease (qurrata aʿun), and make us leaders of the God-conscious.'"[18]

- [A12/A12'] - Just as Maryam ﷺ had never physically touched others (bashr), she later vowed to not even verbally address others (al-bashr). We also learn that Maryam ﷺ was not unchaste (baghiyyā), same as her mother (baghiyyā).
- [A13/A13'] - The structure ends with the messenger informing Maryam ﷺ that Allah ﷻ will make ʿĪsā ﷺ a miraculous sign (āyah) for people. The parallel verses show the manifestation of that miracle as ʿĪsā ﷺ speaks from the cradle to defend his mother's honor.

Upon closer examination, we find that Sections [A12'] and [A13'] also form their own individual mirror structures. [A12'] appears to be organized as so:

A12.1 - But if you see any of the people, say, 'I have vowed silence to the Most Compassionate, so I am not talking to anyone today.'" (26)
A12.2 - Then she returned to her people, carrying him.
A12.3 - They said [in shock], "O Maryam! You have certainly done a horrible thing! (27) **A12.3'** - O sister of Hārūn! Your father was not an indecent man, nor was your mother unchaste." (28)
A12.2' - So, she pointed to the baby.
A12.1' - They exclaimed, "How can we talk to someone who is an infant in the cradle?" (29)

Connections

- [A12.1/A12.1'] - Maryam ﷺ taking a vow to not speak (ukallima) to anyone is paired with her people being frustrated that they are being asked to talk to (nukallimu) a child in the cradle, whom they presume cannot speak.
- [A12.2/A12.2'] - Both parts describe Maryam ﷺ interacting with her baby
- [A12.3/A12.3'] - The center of the structure focuses on the shock of

18 25:47 - وَٱلَّذِينَ يَقُولُونَ رَبَّنَا هَبْ لَنَا مِنْ أَزْوَٰجِنَا وَذُرِّيَّٰتِنَا قُرَّةَ أَعْيُنٍ وَٱجْعَلْنَا لِلْمُتَّقِينَ إِمَامًا

her people upon seeing her with a newborn. They call her by two different names, and state that she has done a "horrible thing." The horrible thing isn't detailed, but the context clues in the paired verse give us an idea of what they were implying.

And [A13'] is structured as follows:

A13.1 - "ʿĪsā' declared, "I am truly a servant of Allah.
 A13.2 - He has given me the Scripture
  A13.3 - and made me a prophet. (30) He has made me a blessing wherever I go,
   A13.4 - and bid me to establish prayer and give alms-tax as long as I live, (31)
   A13.4' - and to be kind to my mother.
  A13.3' - He has not made me arrogant or defiant. (32)
 A13.2' - Safety and protection are with me the day I was born, the day I die, and the day I will be raised back to life!" (33)
A13.1' - That is ʿĪsā, the son of Maryam –

Connections

- [A13.1/A13.1'] - 'Īsā's role is made very clear through the pairing of the outsides of this mirror structure. ʿĪsā عليه السلام was an honorable servant of Allah ﷻ, not a god.
- [A13.2/A13.2'] - By virtue of ʿĪsā عليه السلام following guidance from Scripture, he will have "as-Salām" at all points in life, including the hereafter. As the author explained previously, salām is a comprehensive word that means ʿĪsā عليه السلام will be protected from Satan, the punishments of the grave, and the trials of the Day of Judgment.
- [A13.3/A13.3'] - ʿĪsā عليه السلام tells us two things he has and hasn't been made by Allah ﷻ. He was made (jaʿalanī) a prophet and blessing wherever he goes and was not made (lam yajʿalnī) arrogant and defiant.
- [A13.4/A13.4'] - The center informs of us two different timelines for the tasks of ʿĪsā عليه السلام. He is to establish prayer and give alms-tax for as long as he lives, but being dutiful to his mother was not cut off by his death. One reason mentioned for this is that this is him prophesying that he'd outlive his mother, which is especially true if we take into consideration his second coming.

Before moving to the final structure of Section [A], there are some notable parallels between the narratives of Zakariyyā and Yaḥyā 🕮 and Maryam and ʿĪsā 🕮.[19]

Parallels Between Zakariyyā and Yaḥyā 🕮 and Maryam and ʿĪsā 🕮

As we will see, there are many interesting parallels between the first two stories of this Sūrah. The similarities, which occur in the same order, are summarized in the table below:

---

19   The following parallels are built on the work of Bilal Gökkir in *Form and Structure of Sura Maryam: A Study From Unity of Sura Perspective*

Zakariyyā and Yaḥyā	Maryam and ʿĪsā
"[This is] a mention (dhikr) of the mercy of your Lord to His servant Zakariyyā" (2)	"And mention (wa-dhkur) in the Book [the story of] Maryam" (16)
Went into seclusion to pray	Went into seclusion to worship
Zakariyyā was afraid for the future of his family	Maryam was afraid for her honor
Zakariyyā asks to be gifted (hab-lī) a child and is granted one (ghulām)	Maryam is told that she is being gifted (ahaba-laki) a child (ghulām)
"How can I have a child (annā yakūnu lī ghulāmun)..." (8)	"How can I have a child (annā yakūnu lī ghulāmun)..." (20)
Zakariyyā gives two reasons he shouldn't be able to conceive a child	Maryam gives two reasons why she shouldn't be able to be pregnant
"[An angel] said, "Thus [it will be]; your Lord says, 'It is easy for Me' (qāla kadhālika qāla rabbuka huwa 'alayya hayyin)" (9)	"[The angel] said, "Thus [it will be]; your Lord says, 'It is easy for Me' (qāla kadhāliki qāla rabbuka huwa 'alayya hayyin)" (21)
Allah says He created Zakariyyā from non-existence	Maryam wishes she never existed and was forgotten
Zakariyyā asks for a sign (āyah) and is told he won't speak to people for three nights	Maryam doesn't ask, but is given 'Īsā as a sign (āyah) and told to take a vow of silence for the day
"So, he went out to his people (fa-kharja 'alā qawmihi)..." (11)	"So, she went to her people (fa-atat bihi qawmahā)..." (27)
Zakariyyā signaled to his people	Maryam pointed to her child
Yaḥyā was told to hold firmly to the Scripture (al-Kitāb)	'Īsā was given the Scripture (al- Kitāb)
Yaḥyā was given wisdom as a child	ʿĪsā was given prophethood as a child
Yaḥyā was given kindness and tenderness from Allah	ʿĪsā was made blessed wherever he went by Allah
Yaḥyā was God-conscious	ʿĪsā was ordered to pray and tell others to pray
Yaḥyā was pure (zakāt)	ʿĪsā was ordered to give the purifying dues (al-zakāt) and teach others to give it
"And dutiful to his parents, and he was not a disobedient tyrant (wabarran biwālidayhi walam yakun jabbāran 'aṣīyyan)" (14)	"And dutiful to my mother. He has not made me arrogant or defiant (wabarran biwālidatī walam yaj'alnī jabbāran shaqīyyan)" (32)
"And safety and protection are with him the day he was born and the day he dies and the day he is raised alive (wasalāmun 'alayhi yawma wulida wayawma yamūtu wayawma yub'athu ḥayyā)" (15)	"Safety and protection are with me the day I was born, the day I die, and the day I will be raised back to life (was-salāmu 'alayya yawma wulittu wayawma amūtu wayawma ab'athu ḥayyā)" (33)

The parallels in this outline may inform us of a few points that were not readily apparent upon first reading. For example, notice that Yaḥyā ﷺ being given wisdom as a child lines up with ʿĪsā ﷺ being made a prophet. This may support the opinion that the "wisdom" given to Yaḥyā ﷺ was foreshadowing his eventual prophethood.

Or we can look at what did not align. For example, notice that the verses describing Maryam's pains of labor and childbirth lack an equivalent in the story of Yaḥyā ﷺ. This could be a subtle point being made for us to appreciate the magnitude of child bearing and delivery. In other words, there is nothing to compare it to.

On a broader level, it seems that Allah ﷻ juxtaposes these two stories so closely together to drive home the message coming up in the final structure of Section [A], that is, Allah ﷻ never has, and never will, have a child. The miraculous birth of ʿĪsā ﷷ is very similar to the divine intervention involved with the birth of Yaḥyā ﷷ. Both were amazing prophets, but no more than that. It doesn't make sense to attribute divine properties to ʿĪsā ﷷ when Yaḥyā ﷷ has such a similar story.

Returning to Section [A]

The final part of Section [A] contains another parallel structure, but this one focuses on the consequences of blasphemy and attributing a son to Allah ﷻ.

A14 - the word of truth about which they are in dispute. (34)

  A15 - It is not [befitting] for Allah to take a son; exalted is He!

    A16 - When He decrees an affair, He only says to it, "Be," and it is. (35)

      A17 - ['Īsā said], "And indeed, Allah is my Lord and your Lord, so worship Him. That is a straight path." (36)

A14' - Then the factions differed [concerning 'Īsā] from among them,

  A15' - so woe to those who disbelieved – from the scene of a tremendous Day. (37) How [clearly] they will hear and see the Day they come to Us, but the wrongdoers today are in clear error. (38)

    A16' - And warn them, [O Muhammad], of the Day of Regret, when the matter will be concluded; and [yet], they are in [a state of] heedlessness, and they do not believe. (39)

      A17' - Indeed, it is We who will inherit the earth and whoever is on it, and to Us they will be returned. (40)

Connections

- [A14/A14'] - The structure begins with a declarative statement about ʿĪsā (as) as it is his account "about which they are in dispute." The parallel verse begins along the same vein mentioning that "the factions differed [concerning 'Īsā]."
- [A15/A15'] - Allah ﷻ definitively declares Himself free of the attribution of a son, and to compliment that statement, the corresponding verses allude to the state of those who do not desist from making such claims. They will clearly "hear and see" the truth when they stand before Allah ﷻ on the Day of Judgment. What's more, Allah ﷻ describes these people as being "in clear error (ḍalāl)," which is

a callback to Sūrah al-Fātiḥah wherein many scholars say that the "astray (aḍ-ḍāllīn)" mentioned at the end of the Sūrah is referring to the Christians; the group directly associated with claiming ʿĪsā as a son to Allah ﷻ. [20]

- [A16/A16'] - These two parts are connected through their shared usage of vocabulary. In the top verse, Allah ﷻ begins it saying, "When He decrees an affair (idhā qaḍā amran)" which is similar to the parallel verse in which He says, "when the matter will be decreed (idh quḍiya al-amr)." This creates a link between Allah's ability to decree matters at will without the need for a son, and the fate of those who do not internalize that message.
- [A17/A17'] - Finally, the structure ends with a comprehensive summary of what every prophet and messenger was sent to teach: Allah ﷻ is our Master, so worship Him and accept His guidance. Why? Because we will all be brought back to Him for accounting and judgment.

Integrative Coherence of Section [A]

Besides the numerous parallels between the stories of Zakariyyā ﷺ and Maryam ﷺ outlined above, there are other, more subtle, anchors and motifs running through this Sūrah that help to create a sense of unity and coherence.

The Sūrah began with Zakariyyā ﷺ calling out (nādā) to his Master in a lowered voice (nidā'an khafiyyā). When we read the story of Maryam ﷺ giving birth we learn that a voice called out (nādā) to her, but the details of how she was called are omitted. Maybe it is the case that Allah ﷻ used the same verb here as with Zakariyyā ﷺ to hint that Maryam ﷺ was spoken to in a comforting and lowered voice, such that no one else could hear.

When Zakariyyā ﷺ prays for a child he asks that he is gifted (hab-lī) it. This mirrors what the messenger said to Maryam ﷺ when he said that he has come to gift her (ahab la-kī) a child. This again echoes the prayer for children we touched on earlier from Sūrah al-Furqān which states, "And those who say, 'Our Master, gift us (hab lanā) from our spouses and children those who

20 Ibn Jarīr aṭ-Ṭabarī, Tafsīr aṭ-Ṭabarī, 1:7

put our heart at ease, and make us leaders of the God-conscious.'" [21]

When praying for a child, Zakariyyā ﷺ adds that he would like his offspring to "inherit from me and inherit from the family of Yaʿqūb (yarithunī wayarithu min āli Yaʿqūb)" which is similar to what Allah ﷻ says to conclude the Section, "Indeed, it is We who will inherit the earth and whoever is on it (Innā narithu al-arḍa waman 'alayhā)." We may inherit things while on this earth, but ultimately everything will return to its original owner, Allah ﷻ.

Finally, we see that the theme of being God-conscious (taqiyyā) runs throughout the Sūrah. For this current comparison, we find it used to describe Yaḥyā ﷺ, and in the desperate outcry of Maryam ﷺ when the mysterious messenger approached her. Again, this ties into the very comprehensive prayer for children wherein we say, "And those who say, 'Our Master, gift us from our spouses and children those who put our heart at ease, and make us leaders of the God-conscious (muttaqīna).'" [22]

Section (B) - Ibrāhīm and His Father

The following section can be further broken down into its own mirror composition:

B1 - And mention in the Book [the story of] Ibrāhīm. Indeed, he was a man of truth and a prophet. (41) [Mention] when he said to his father, "O my father, why do you worship that which does not hear and does not see and will not benefit you at all? (42) O my father, indeed there has come to me of knowledge that which has not come to you, so follow me; I will guide you to an even path. (43) O my father, do not worship Satan. Indeed, Satan has ever been, to the Most Merciful, disobedient. (44) O my father, indeed I fear that there will touch you a punishment from the Most Merciful so you would be to Satan a companion [in Hellfire]." (45) [His father] said, "Have you no desire for my gods, O Ibrāhīm? If you do not desist, I will surely stone you, so avoid me a prolonged time." (46)

> **B2** - [Ibrāhīm] said, "I pray for your safety and security. I will ask forgiveness for you of my Lord. Indeed, He is ever gracious to me. (47) And I will leave you and those you invoke other than Allah
>
> **B2'** - and will invoke my Lord. I expect that I will not be in invocation to my Lord unhappy." (48) So, when he had left them and those they worshipped other than Allah,

B1' - We gave him Isḥāq and Ya'qūb, and each [of them] We made a prophet. (49) And We gave them of Our mercy, and we made for them a reputation of high honor. (50)

Summarized another way, it looks like this:

21 25:47 - وَٱلَّذِينَ يَقُولُونَ رَبَّنَا هَبْ لَنَا مِنْ أَزْوَٰجِنَا وَذُرِّيَّٰتِنَا قُرَّةَ أَعْيُنٍ وَٱجْعَلْنَا لِلْمُتَّقِينَ إِمَامًا

22 Ibid.

B1 - Losing Connection to Father (41-46)
B2 – Leaving family (47-48a)
B2' – Leaving community (48b)
B1' – Granted Children and Grandchildren (49-50)

Connections

- [B1/B1'] - Ibrāhīm ﷺ is tested with his father's polytheism and tries his best to present logical arguments to his father before ultimately being rejected. This is paired with Allah's reward for Ibrāhīm ﷺ wherein he is given the good news of not only children, but even grandchildren. And similar to Ibrāhīm ﷺ who was "truthful (ṣiddīqā)" and "a prophet (nabiyyā)", his descendants are also described as "prophets (nabiyyā)" and as having an "honorable mention (lisāna ṣidqin 'aliyyā)" which suggests that his lineage will carry on his legacy of monotheism. He lost a father, but gained so much more.
- [B2/B2'] - The section centers on Ibrāhīm ﷺ declaring himself free of his family and community, specifically with regards to their polytheistic practices. Both parts consist of a prayer from Ibrāhīm ﷺ and him leaving them.

If we break the section down further, we will see that [B1] contains a ring structure with the argument of Ibrāhīm ﷺ embedded in the middle as a parallel structure:

B1.1 - And mention in the Book [the story of] Ibrāhīm. Indeed, he was a man of truth and a prophet. (41)
B1.2 - [Mention] when he said to his father, "My dear father, why do you worship that which does not hear and does not see and will not benefit you at all? (42) My dear father, indeed there has come to me of knowledge that which has not come to you, so follow me; I will guide you to an even path. (43) My dear father, do not worship Satan. Indeed, Satan has ever been, to the Most Merciful, disobedient. (44) My dear father, indeed I fear that there will touch you a punishment from the Most Merciful so you would be to Satan a companion [in Hellfire]." (45)
B.1' - [His father] said, "Have you no desire for my gods, O Ibrāhīm? If you do not desist, I will surely stone you, so avoid me a prolonged time." (46)

Summarized another way:

PROPHETHOOD: And mention in the Book [the story of] Ibrāhīm. Indeed, he was a man of truth and a prophet. (41)
WORSHIP: [Mention] when he said to his father, "My dear father, why do you worship that which does not hear and does not see and will not benefit you at all? (42)
RATIONALE: My dear father, indeed there has come to me of knowledge that which has not come to you, so follow me; I will guide you to an even path. (43)
WORSHIP: My dear father, do not worship Satan. Indeed, Satan has ever been, to the Most Merciful, disobedient. (44)
RATIONALE: My dear father, indeed I fear that there will touch you a punishment from the Most Merciful so you would be to Satan a companion [in Hellfire]." (45)
REJECTING IDOLS: [His father] said, "Have you no desire for my gods, O Ibrāhīm? If you do not desist, I will surely stone you, so avoid me a prolonged time." (46)

Connections

- [B1.1/B1.1'] - The intro tells us who Ibrāhīm عليه السلام is; a man of truth and a prophet of Allah سبحانه وتعالى. The corresponding conclusion shows Ibrāhīm's commitment to prophethood and monotheism as he is outcast by his own father because he "has no desire" for their fake gods.
- [B1.2] - At the center lies the beautiful argument of Ibrāhīm عليه السلام to his father. Each sentence begins with "My dear father," to emphasize the care behind the words to come. Ibrāhīm عليه السلام begins twice with a statement about the irrationality behind worshiping (ta'bud) other than Allah سبحانه وتعالى, and twice he provides his rationale for saying what could be perceived as harsh words to his father. In both cases, he acknowledges that Allah سبحانه وتعالى has given him knowledge of the unseen that his father could not be privy to without guidance.

[B2] and [B2'], the center of Section [B] which describe Ibrāhīm عليه السلام leaving his people, is also set up in a parallel structure:

B2.1 - [Ibrāhīm] said, "I pray for your safety and security. I will ask forgiveness for you of my Lord. Indeed, He is ever gracious to me. (47)
B2.2 - And I will leave you and those you invoke other than Allah
B2.1' - and will invoke my Lord. I expect that I will not be in invocation to my Lord unhappy." (48)
B2.2' - So when he had left them and those they worshipped other than Allah,

Connections

- [B2.1/B2.1'] - Both halves begin in the same manner, with Ibrāhīm (as) praying to his Lord, and Ibrāhīm عليه السلام adding in both instances a point of optimism about his prayer being fulfilled.

- [B2.2/B2.2'] - Both halves also end the same way with Ibrāhīm leaving his family and community with almost the same wording in Arabic, "And I will leave you and those you invoke other than Allah (waaʿtazilukum wamā tadʿūna min dūnil-lāhi)" versus "He had left them and those they worshipped other than Allah (iʿtazalahum wamā yadʿūna min dūnil-lāhi)."

[B1'], the conclusion of Section [B], is also set up as a parallel structure:

B1.3 - We gifted him Isḥāq and Ya'qūb,
B1.4 - and each [of them] We made a prophet. (49)
B1.3' - And We gifted them of Our mercy,
B1.4' - and we made for them a reputation of high honor. (50)

Connections

- [B1.3/B1.3'] - Both parts begin with Allah saying "We gifted (wahabnā)" something to Ibrāhīm and his family.
- [B1.4/B1.4'] - Both parallels conclude with Allah saying, "We made (jaʿalnā)..." in reference to the family of Ibrāhīm.

Integrative Coherence of Section [B]

Now that we've broken down Section [B] into its individual parts, we can take a step back and observe how the Section fits seamlessly within the larger Sūrah.

Recall that one of the main themes of this Sūrah is that of monotheism, with 'Īsā's alleged divinity being of particular interest. As we will continuously see throughout the Sūrah, Allah draws comparisons of ʿĪsā with other prophets in order to demonstrate that the miraculous events and special status he was granted make him a prophet, but nothing grander.

For example, in Section [B], Allah says that Ibrāhīm was a "prophet (nabiyyā)" and also says about Isḥāq and Yaʿqūb that, "We made them prophets (jaʿalnā nabiyyā)." This is almost the same wording used when ʿĪsā introduced himself declaring that Allah had, "made me a prophet (jaʿalanī nabiyyā)."

We also find that both Sections mention the prayer of safety and security (salām). Yaḥyā and ʿĪsā ﵇ were granted safety and security on the day of their births, deaths and resurrections. Ibrāhīm ﵇ uses the same prayer when leaving his father.

Another interesting parallel lay in the prayers of Zakariyyā ﵇ and Ibrāhīm ﵇. Both conclude their prayers to Allah ﷾ with almost the same wording. Zakariyyā ﵇ says, "...and I have never been disappointed in my supplication to You, my Lord (walam akun biduʿāika rabbi shaqiyyā)" while Ibrāhīm ﵇ is recorded to have said, "...I will never be disappointed in invoking my Lord (lā akūna biduʿāi rabbī shaqiyyā)." This again lends itself to the fulfillment of Allah's gift to Ibrāhīm ﵇ wherein He granted him a lineage - Zakariyyā ﵇ is a descendant on the side of Isḥāq ﵇ - that would hold on to monotheism.

Continuing the comparisons between Zakariyyā and Ibrāhīm ﵇, we find that both wanted their family to be an ally (waliyy) of Allah ﷾. Zakariyyā ﵇ asks that his child be a successor to him (waliyy), and by extension, an ally to Allah ﷾. Ibrāhīm ﵇ fears for his father's future as an idol worshiper so he warns his father that he's on course to become an ally (waliyy) of the Shaytan if he doesn't turn back to Allah ﷾.

We also find a similarity between Yaḥyā and Ibrāhīm ﵇. Allah ﷾ describes Yaḥyā ﵇ as not being "disobedient ('aṣiyyā)," which is the same wording used when Ibrāhīm ﵇ says to his father, "Do not worship Satan. Satan has always been, to the Most Merciful, disobedient ('aṣiyyā)." The description of Yaḥyā ﵇, therefore, has a possible supplement later in the Sūrah. If one is not worshiping Allah ﷾ then they may be in danger of worshiping Satan.

Our final example of integrative coherence for this Section is an interesting one between Ibrāhīm ﵇ and Maryam ﵇. Both use the idea of being "touched" in a negative connotation, but juxtapose it with the mention of Allah's name, The Most Merciful (ar-Raḥmān). When the stranger walked in on Maryam ﵇ she said, "I seek refuge with the Most Merciful (ar-Raḥmān) from you if you were God-conscious!" She is then informed of her miraculous pregnancy at which point she remarks, "How can I have a child when no man has touched me (yamsas-nī)?" This sense of fear and anxiety, mixed with hope in the Most Merciful is repeated when Ibrāhīm ﵇ kindly tells his father, "I certainly fear that a punishment will touch you (yamassa-ka) from the Most Merciful (ar-Raḥmān)."

And thus concludes our analysis of Section [B]. Hopefully we are already getting an appreciation for the remarkable coherence and structure to Allah's words.

Section [C] - Our Forefathers in Faith

Section [C] mentions many prophets of the past in what may appear to be a haphazard list. When we examine this Section more closely, we will find that not only does the list form a ring structure, but that every prophet mentioned ties into the overarching themes of this Sūrah.

Below is the proposed ring structure of Section [C][23]:

C1 - And mention in the Book, Mūsā. Indeed, he was especially chosen, and he was a messenger and a prophet. (51) And We called him from the side of the mount at [his] right and brought him near, confiding [to him]. (52) And We gifted him out of Our mercy his brother Hārūn as a prophet. (53)

> **C2** - And mention in the Book, Ismāʿīl. Indeed, he was true to his promise, and he was a messenger and a prophet. (54) And he used to enjoin on his people prayer and the purifying dues and was to his Lord pleasing. (55)
>
> > **C3** - And mention in the Book, Idrīs. Indeed, he was a man of truth and a prophet. (56) And We raised him to a high station. (57)
> >
> > > **C4** - Those were the ones upon whom Allah bestowed favor from among the prophets of the descendants of Ādam
> >
> > **C3'** - and of those We carried [in the ship] with Nūḥ,
>
> **C2'** - and of the descendants of Ibrāhīm

C1' - and Isrāīl, and of those whom We guided and chose. When the verses of the Most Merciful were recited to them, they bowed their heads to the ground, weeping. (58)

Connections

- [C1/C1'] - The descendants of Isrāīl (also known as Yaʿqūb) are paired with Mūsā and Hārūn. This is appropriate as the story of Yaʿqūb moving to Egypt to be with his son, Yūsūf, is a precursor to the story of Mūsā and Hārūn being slaves in Egypt and facing the Pharaoh. Additionally, Mūsā was "especially chosen (mukhlaṣ)" to be a prophet, which is similar to those whom Allah "chose (ijtabay-nā)" to be guided. The different Arabic word for "choosing" utilized for Mūsā may be Allah demonstrating Mūsā's elevated rank.

23 The following observations are built off the work done by: Khan, Nouman. S. Maryam Structure Party Part 4. Facebook, 23 August, 2019, https://www.facebook.com/noumanbayyinah/videos/441726859765230/. Accessed 1 February, 2020

- The next part of the beginning verses then mentions Mūsā's interaction with Allah 🕮. The details are given in other parts of the Quran, but if we look to the corresponding verse in [C1'], we find the most relevant information; Mūsā 🕮 had verses of the Most Merciful told to him by Allah 🕮 Himself.

- The final parallel appears to be between Mūsā 🕮 being "gifted out of [Allah's] mercy, his brother Hārūn," and the believers bowing their heads to the ground in humility. Mūsā's reaction to having received his brother as a partner in prophecy is not given in the Quran. Though, if we pair the two aforementioned parts together, then maybe we have a hint to Mūsā's humbling and tear-filled reply.

- [C2/C2'] - Here, the descendants of Ibrāhīm 🕮 are paired with Ismā'īl 🕮. For the original Arab audience, this was an important reminder that they, as distant children of Ismā'īl 🕮, are actually from the lineage of Ibrāhīm 🕮 and should therefore possess the most zeal for reestablishing his legacy of pure monotheism.

- [C3/C3'] - As we move towards the center of this Section, we find the first mention of prophets who pre-date Ibrāhīm 🕮, as Idrīs 🕮 and Nūh 🕮 come paired together. Both prophets here share some connection to Ādam 🕮. As explained by the author above, Idrīs 🕮 is considered the first prophet sent after Ādam 🕮, while Nūh 🕮 is nicknamed the "second father of mankind," with Ādam 🕮 being the obvious first.

- [C4] - At the center and focal point of this section and Sūrah, we have the first human, Ādam 🕮. Similar to 'Īsā 🕮, he was created without a father (or even a mother), but also like 'Īsā 🕮, his miraculous creation doesn't raise his ranks higher than a prophet (nabiyy) just as 'Īsā 🕮 was called earlier.

Integrative Coherence of Section [C]

As mentioned earlier, the prophets in this Section may appear random, but besides being placed in the list in a structured manner, there is also an integrative relevance to each of their examples.

1.

Mūsā 🕮 - He went into seclusion to speak to Allah 🕮, just as Zakariyyā

﵇ and Maryam ﵇ did, and was "gifted (wahabnā)" his brother to aid him. Again, this is similar to the family Zakariyyā and Maryam ﵇ were "gifted" after their seclusions.

Mūsā ﵇ was also called out to by Allah ﷻ (nādaynā-hu) in the same way Zakariyyā ﵇ called out (nādā) softly to Allah ﷻ and how Maryam ﵇ was called (nādā-hā) from below her. Like in the case of Maryam ﵇ where the details of how this call sounded was omitted, this might be another subtle hint that Allah ﷻ called out to Mūsā ﵇ in a quiet and calm fashion as to not startle him.

2.

Ismāʿīl ﵇ - We learned about Ibrāhīm's test with his father in the previous Section. Here we find mention of his test with his son when Ibrāhīm ﵇ was commanded to sacrifice Ismāʿīl ﵇. Ismāʿīl ﵇ is also described with the qualities of commanding his people to pray and give their purifying dues (aṣ-Ṣalāh wa al-Zakāh), same as ʿĪsā ﵇ was related to do (aṣ-Ṣalāh wa al-Zakāh). Allah ﷻ also informs us that Ismā'īl ﵇ was "pleasing (marḍiyyā)," which echoes the prayer of Zakariyyā ﵇ when he asked that his son, Yaḥyā ﵇, be "pleasing (raḍiyyā)."

3.

Idrīs ﵇ - There is little known about Idrīs ﵇, but what Allah ﷻ tells us here connects to the Sūrah's context. Idrīs ﵇ was "a man of truth and a prophet (ṣiddīqan nabiyyā)" same as Ibrāhīm ﵇ (ṣiddīqan nabiyyā). He was also "raised to a high rank (rafaʿnā-hu makānan ʿaliyyā)," which echoes what Allah ﷻ said about ʿĪsā ﵇ in Sūrah Āl ʿImrān, "I will take you back and raise you up (rāfiʿu-ka) to Me."[24]

4.

Ādam ﵇ - He is the prophet with the most explicit connection to ʿĪsā ﵇, as Allah ﷻ says in Sūrah Āl ʿImrān, "Indeed, the example of ʿĪsā to Allah is like that of Ādam. He created Him from dust; then He said to him, 'Be,' and he was."[25] It is thus very appropriate that Ādam ﵇ sits at the center of

24 3:55 - إِنِّي مُتَوَفِّيكَ وَرَافِعُكَ إِلَيَّ

25 3:59 - إِنَّ مَثَلَ عِيسَىٰ عِندَ اللَّهِ كَمَثَلِ آدَمَ ۖ خَلَقَهُ مِن تُرَابٍ ثُمَّ قَالَ لَهُ كُن فَيَكُونُ

this Sūrah since he is the progenitor of monotheism on this earth and of all children.

5.

Nūh عليه السلام - His example provides a complimentary image of the family of Zakariyyā عليه السلام, as Nūh's wife and child ended up rebelling against Allah ﷾.[26]

6.

Ibrāhīm عليه السلام - The entire section before this current one was concerning him and the monotheism he was trying to spread. Interestingly, elsewhere in the Quran, Ibrāhīm عليه السلام was also given good news of offspring in his old age. And mimicking the prayer of Zakariyyā عليه السلام, Ibrāhīm's wife shockingly asked, "How am I to bear a child when I am an old woman, and my husband here is an old man?"[27]

7.

Israīl عليه السلام - The original twelve children of Israīl عليه السلام provide a comprehensive view of how believing children may turn out. Some will be obedient from the beginning, such as Yūsuf عليه السلام and Binyāmīn, and others might disobey and act out, but so long as their faith is intact, they will return to Allah's obedience eventually.

As we have just observed, each prophet mentioned has some tie-in to the running motifs of family, the alleged divinity of Christ, and pure monotheism.

---

26 Interestingly, Allah ﷾ worded this verse saying, "Those were the ones upon whom Allah bestowed favor from among the prophets of the descendants of Ādam and of those We carried [in the ship] with Nūh, and of the descendants of Ibrāhīm and Israīl..."

Notice that Allah ﷾ broke up the list of those favored from the "descendants" when it came to Nūh عليه السلام. This is appropriate since we learn in other places in the Quran that his wife disbelieved in him and his son disobeyed him at the crucial moment. In other words, his descendants weren't the ones who carried Islam to the next generation. It was the believers who Allah ﷾ "carried [in the ship] with Nūh."

This is a simple example of Allah's precision and accuracy in word choice.

27 11:71-72 - وَامْرَأَتُهُ قَائِمَةٌ فَضَحِكَتْ فَبَشَّرْنَاهَا بِإِسْحَاقَ وَمِن وَرَاءِ إِسْحَاقَ يَعْقُوبَ * قَالَتْ يَا وَيْلَتَىٰ أَأَلِدُ وَأَنَا عَجُوزٌ وَهَٰذَا بَعْلِي شَيْخًا ۖ إِنَّ هَٰذَا لَشَيْءٌ عَجِيبٌ

Section [B'] - Path to Salvation

The next section focuses on our method of salvation in the Hereafter, and the choices we have in obtaining it. We can choose to take the path of misguidance, or we can choose guidance and obedience to Allah ﷻ and reap the benefits. When the contents of Section [B'] are organized, it appears to form a simple ring structure:

B3 - But there came after them successors who neglected prayer and pursued desires; so, they are going to meet evil - (59)
B4 - Except those who repent, believe and do righteousness;
B5 - for those will enter Paradise and will not be wronged at all. (60) [Therein are] gardens of perpetual residence which the Most Merciful has promised His servants in the unseen. Indeed, His promise has ever been coming. (61) They will not hear therein any ill speech - only [greetings of] perfection - and they will have their provision therein, morning and afternoon. (62) That is Paradise, which We give as inheritance
B4' - to those of Our servants who were fearing of Allah. (63)
B3' - [Jibrīl said], "And we [angels] descend not except by the order of your Lord. To Him belongs that before us and that behind us and what is in between. And never is your Lord forgetful - (64) Lord of the heavens and the earth and whatever is between them - so worship Him and have patience for His worship. Do you know of any similarity to Him?" (65)

Summarized another way, it appears as so:

B3 – Choosing Misguidance
B4 – Actions for Salvation
B5 – Ultimate reward of Salvation
B4' – Characteristic for Salvation
B3' – Choosing Guidance

Connections

- [B3/B3'] - The ring begins and ends with two very contrasting groups. The first leave off prayer and choose to follow their desires while the latter are described as obedient to the commands of Allah ﷻ. Unlike the disbelievers, the believer will "worship Him" and will be perseverant with their acts of worship.
- [B4/B4'] - These two parts give a summarized view of one who is primed for salvation and reward on the Day of Judgment. It is a combination of outward actions and internal recognition of Allah ﷻ in all one does.
- [B5] - The center describes the incredible reward in store for those

who embody the aforementioned qualities. Choose guidance over misguidance, act accordingly, and Paradise will be your reward by Allah's mercy and permission.

Integrative Coherence of Section [B']

Though a relatively short section, Section [B'] has many anchors which relate it back to the surrounding context.

Allah ﷻ described the ones who call Christ a god saying, "Then the factions differed from among them (fakhtalafa al-aḥzābu min bayni-him)...," which is very similar to the Arabic of how this Section began, "But there came after them successors (fakhalafa min baʿdi-him khalfun)..." drawing a possible connection between these two groups.

In the previous section, Ismāʿīl ﷺ is described as, "true to his promise (ṣādiqal waʿdi)," which ties into the "promise (waʿd)" of Paradise which Allah ﷻ "promised (waʿada)" for the believers. If Ismāʿīl ﷺ fulfilled his promise, what could possibly be said of the word of Allah ﷻ other than that it is "sure to come"?

For the fourth and final time in this Sūrah, we find usage of a derivative of "salām." It has been used to describe Yaḥyā ﷺ and ʿĪsā ﷺ in their birth, death and afterlife, and Ibrāhīm ﷺ used it to say goodbye to his father. Here we see its culmination as it is used to describe Paradise, the place free of all faults and deficiencies (salāmā).

We find another connection to Paradise in the usage of "morning and afternoon (bukratan waʿashiyyā)." Earlier in the Sūrah, Zakariyyā ﷺ signaled to his people to "exalt [Allah] in the morning and afternoon (bukratan waʿashiyyā)," and here we are informed that the inhabitants of Paradise will "have their provisions therein, morning and afternoon (bukratan waʿashiyyā)," which gives us a possible link to the reward for praising Allah ﷻ in this life.

Again, in this Sūrah, we find a reference to inheritance. Earlier Zakariyyā ﷺ prayed for a child to inherit from him (yarithunī wayarithu min āli Yaʿqūba). Later, Allah ﷻ tells us that He is the One "who will inherit the earth and whoever is on it (Innā narithu al-arḍa waman ʿalay-hā)." In this section though, we are told of the best inheritance for a believer. The previous two references speak of a worldly inheritance, but Allah ﷻ then tells us, "That is Paradise, which We give as inheritance to those of Our servants who were conscious [of Allah] (tilka al-jannatu al-latī nūrithu min 'ibādinā man kāna taqiyyā)."

Next is an interesting connection between Maryam 🌸 giving birth and a description of Allah 🕌. When Maryam 🌸 was in the worst moments of childbirth she cried out that she wished she was "long forgotten (nasyan mansiyā)." Using the same verbal root, in this Section, Jibrīl 🌸 says that "your Master has never been forgetful (nasiyā)." This gives us a possible correlation between being in a desperate situation and not being "forgotten" by Allah 🕌. Interestingly, in the verse immediately after her cry for help, Maryam 🌸 is given miraculous help from an untold source. Maybe it is the same one who spoke these words here.

The final example has to do with names. After Zakariyyā's prayer he was given the good news of a child named Yaḥyā which Allah 🕌 had "not assigned to any before [this] name (samiyā)." In this Section, Jibrīl 🌸 asks, "Do you know of any, for Him, similarity (samiyā)?" While there were none named Yaḥyā "before" his birth, there are certainly those with his name now. But the same is not true of Allah 🕌. None have, nor will, be called Allah 🕌 except the One, True God.

And thus ends our analysis of Section [B'].

Section [A'] - Denying the True Reality

The final Section of this Sūrah is one of the lengthiest, and thus contains multiple sub-sections within it. Overall, it appears this section can be summarized into a simple ring structure as so:

A18 – And the disbeliever says, "When I have died, am I going to be brought forth alive?" (66) Does man not remember that We created him before, while he was nothing? (67) So, by your Lord, We will surely gather them and the devils; then We will bring them to be present around Hell upon their knees. (68) Then We will surely extract from every sect those of them who were worst against the Most Merciful in insolence. (69) Then, surely it is We who are most knowing of those most worthy of burning therein. (70) And there is none of you except he will come to it. This is upon your Lord an inevitability decreed. (71) Then We will save those who feared Allah and leave the wrongdoers within it, on their knees. (72) And when Our verses are recited to them as clear evidences, those who disbelieve say to those who believe, "Which of [our] two parties is best in position and best in association?" (73) And how many a generation have We destroyed before them who were better in possessions and [outward] appearance? (74)

A19 – Say, "Whoever is in error - let the Most Merciful extend for him an extension [in wealth and time] until, when they see that which they were promised - either punishment [in this world] or the Hour [of resurrection] - they will come to know who is worst in position and weaker in soldiers." (75) And Allah increases those who were guided, in guidance, and the enduring good deeds are better to your Lord for reward and better for recourse. (76) Then, have you seen he who disbelieved in Our verses and said, "I will surely be given wealth and children [in the next life]?" (77) Has he looked into the unseen, or has he taken from the Most Merciful a promise? (78) No! We will record what he says and extend for him from the punishment extensively. (79) And We will inherit him [in] what he mentions, and he will come to Us alone. (80) And they have taken besides Allah [false] deities that they would be for them [a source of] honor. (81) No! Those "gods" will deny their worship of them and will be against them opponents [on the Day of Judgement]. (82)

A18' – Do you not see that We have sent the devils upon the disbelievers, inciting them to [evil] with [constant] incitement? (83) So be not impatient over them. We only count out to them a [limited] number. (84) On the Day We will gather the righteous to the Most Merciful as a delegation (85) And will drive the criminals to Hell in thirst (86) None will have [power of] intercession except he who had taken from the Most Merciful a covenant. (87) And they say, "The Most Merciful has taken [for Himself] a son." (88) You have done an atrocious thing. (89) The heavens almost rupture therefrom and the earth splits open and the mountains collapse in devastation (90) That they attribute to the Most Merciful a son. (91) And it is not appropriate for the Most Merciful that He should take a son. (92) There is no one in the heavens and earth but that he comes to the Most Merciful as a servant. (93) He has enumerated them and counted them a [full] counting. (94) And all of them are coming to Him on the Day of Resurrection alone. (95) Indeed, those who have believed and done righteous deeds - the Most Merciful will appoint for them affection. (96) So, [O Muhammad], We have only made Qur'an easy in the Arabic language that you may give good tidings thereby to the righteous and warn thereby a hostile people. (97) And how many have We destroyed before them of generations? Do you perceive of them anyone or hear from them a sound? (98)

Connections

- [A18/A18'] - The opening of this ring says that Allah ﷻ "will save those who had God-consciousness (ittaqaw)," but the details of how they will be brought to Allah ﷻ for saving is mentioned in the complementary section when Allah ﷻ says that He "will gather the God-conscious (muttaqīn)" as an "honored delegation."
- The parallel verses also link the disbelievers with the "devils (shayāṭīn)." In the top verses, Allah ﷻ swears to gather the disbelievers and "devils (shayāṭīn)" and repeats the sentiment in the bottom verses when He says that He "sent the devils (shayāṭīn) upon the disbelievers, inciting them to [evil]."
- We also learn that everyone will be brought to observe Hell (wāri-du-hā). Using the same Arabic root, Allah ﷻ says in the parallel section that Allah ﷻ will "drive the criminals to Hell in thirst (wirdan)."
- Both sections conclude in a similar manner. Allah ﷻ rhetorically

asks in [A18], "And how many a generation have We destroyed before them (wa kam ahlaknā qabla-hum min qarnin) who were better in possessions and [outward] appearances?" He ﷻ then repeats the question at the conclusion of the Sūrah saying, "And how many a generation have We destroyed before them (wa kam ahlaknā qabla-hum min qarnin)? Do you perceive any of them or hear from them a sound?" These disbelievers used to boast and feel so proud of their material wealth, but Allah ﷻ so completely removed them from this earth that there are no traces of their grandeur anymore.

- [A19] - At the center we see the reward of the believers sandwiched by the arrogance of the disbelievers. The center is acting like a summary of the surrounding subsections as it touches on the themes of denial, fate, and accounting told in more detail around it.

While the above structuring may seem a bit convoluted at first, the organization becomes much clearer once we break down each subsection into its individual parts. For example, [A18] can be further broken down into its own ring structure:

A18.1 – Denial of Resurrection and Judgment	And the disbeliever says, "When I have died, am I going to be brought forth alive?" (66) Does man not remember that We created him before, while he was nothing? (67) So, by your Lord, We will surely gather them and the devils; then We will bring them to be present around Hell upon their knees. (68) Then We will surely extract from every sect those of them who were worst against the Most Merciful in insolence. (69) Then, surely it is We who are most knowing of those most worthy of burning therein. (70) And there is none of you except he will come to it. This is upon your Lord an inevitability decreed. (71)
A18.2 – Fate	Then We will save those who feared Allah and leave the wrongdoers within it, on their knees. (72)
A18.1' – Denial of Accountability	And when Our verses are recited to them as clear evidences, those who disbelieve say to those who believe, "Which of [our] two parties is best in position and best in association?" (73) And how many a generation have We destroyed before them who were better in possessions and [outward] appearance? (74)

Connections

- [A18.1/A18.1'] - The outsides of the ring describe the denial of all aspects of liability. The disbelievers deny being resurrected after death, they deny being brought for judgment before Allah ﷻ and they deny any type of accountability for their corrupt actions, both in this life and the next.
- [A18.2] - The center mentions the fate of both believers and disbe-

lievers. Those who feared standing before Allah ﷻ on the Day of Judgment, and acted accordingly, will be saved. And those who deny any such accounting will be left kneeling before Hellfire before eventually being thrown in.

Subsection [A19] can also be made into a smaller ring structure:

A19.1 – Reality of Resurrection and Judgment	Say, "Whoever is in error - let the Most Merciful extend for him an extension [in wealth and time] until, when they see that which they were promised - either punishment [in this world] or the Hour [of resurrection] - they will come to know who is worst in position and weaker in soldiers." (75)
A19.2 – Fate of Believers	And Allah increases those who were guided, in guidance, and the enduring good deeds are better to your Lord for reward and better for recourse. (76)
A19.1' – Reality of Accountability	Then, have you seen he who disbelieved in Our verses and said, "I will surely be given wealth and children [in the next life]?" (77) Has he looked into the unseen, or has he taken from the Most Merciful a promise? (78) No! We will record what he says and extend for him from the punishment extensively. (79) And We will inherit him [in] what he mentions, and he will come to Us alone. (80) And they have taken besides Allah [false] deities that they would be for them [a source of] honor. (81) No! Those "gods" will deny their worship of them and will be against them opponents [on the Day of Judgement]. (82)

Connections

- [A19.1/A19.1'] - The ring begins by describing those who were arrogant on account of their superior numbers and wealth. Accordingly, the ring ends with the disbelievers boastfully claiming that they will "surely be given wealth and children [in the next life]." Allah ﷻ utilizes the conclusion of this ring to refute their baseless claim.
- The beginning says that Allah ﷻ will "extend (madd)" the disbelievers in time and wealth to given them a false sense of security. In the corresponding verses, Allah ﷻ says that He will "extend (madd)" the disbelievers in punishment on account of their lies and denial of accounting.
- [A19.2] - The center describes the fate of the believers who presumably did not exhibit the arrogance highlighted in the surrounding text.

And finally, even [A18'] can be made into a ring structure:

A18.3 – Judgment	Do you not see that We have sent the devils upon the disbelievers, inciting them to [evil] with [constant] incitement? (83) So be not impatient over them. We only count out to them a [limited] number. (84) On the Day We will gather the God-conscious to the Most Merciful as a delegation (85) And will drive the criminals to Hell in thirst (86) None will have [power of] intercession except he who had taken from the Most Merciful a covenant. (87)
A18.4 – Great Blasphemy	And they say, "The Most Merciful has taken [for Himself] a son." (88) You have done an atrocious thing. (89) The heavens almost rupture therefrom and the earth splits open and the mountains collapse in devastation (90) That they attribute to the Most Merciful a son. (91) And it is not appropriate for the Most Merciful that He should take a son. (92) There is no one in the heavens and earth but that he comes to the Most Merciful as a servant. (93)
A18.3' – Accountability	He has enumerated them and counted them a [full] counting. (94) And all of them are coming to Him on the Day of Resurrection alone. (95) Indeed, those who have believed and done righteous deeds - the Most Merciful will appoint for them affection. (96) So, [O Muhammad], We have only made Qur'an easy in the Arabic language that you may give good news thereby to the God-conscious and warn thereby a hostile people. (97) And how many have We destroyed before them of generations? Do you perceive of them anyone or hear from them a sound? (98)

Connections

- [A18.3/A18.3'] - The final ring begins by imploring the believers to "not be impatient over [the disbelievers]. We only count them out to a limited number (ʿaddā)." Section [A18.3'] then begins with Allah ﷻ assuring the believers that He "enumerated [the disbelievers] and counted them a [full] accounting (ʿaddā)."
- The "God-conscious (muttaqīn)" are also mentioned at the tail ends of each subsection. The first time is in reference to them being gathered to the Most Merciful and the second time is when the Messenger ﷺ is told that the Quran was revealed in their native tongue in order to "give good news thereby to the God-conscious (muttaqīn)."
- [A18.4] - The center of this ring is a final summary and conclusion of the arguments made against the divinity of Christ. The greatest blasphemy one can commit is to associate partners with Allah ﷻ, and in case the arguments before were too subtle, Allah ﷻ clearly spells out the crime of attributing a son to Him.

Integrative Coherence of [A']

Besides being a coherent whole, Section [A'] also contains many anchors that establish connections back to the previous sections.

For example, after stating that everyone will have to stand and witness Hellfire, Allah ﷻ says this is "an inevitability decreed (maqḍiyā)." When hearing this, the audience recalls the statement of the angel when he told

Maryam 🙵 that her pregnancy was "a matter [already] decreed (maqḍiyā)." This may suggest to the listener that, just as surely that Maryam 🙵 got pregnant and gave birth, they will undoubtedly stand before Hellfire and witness their potential fate.

In Section [A'], Allah 🙵 says that He extends the lives and provisions of the disbelievers until they "see that which they were promised (yūʿadūna)." This recalls the promise (waʿd) of Allah 🙵 given in Section [B'] and the fulfillment of the promise (ṣādiqa al-waʿd) of Ismāʿīl 🙵 in Section [C].

Here we also find the final mention of inheritance. Allah 🙵 says that He will inherit (narithu) all that man leaves behind when he dies, which is a callback to the inheritance Allah 🙵 said He would take at the end of Section [A], "No doubt We will inherit (narithu) the earth and all who are on it."

Towards the end of the Sūrah, Allah 🙵 says "There is no one in the heavens and earth (as-samāwāti wal-arḍi) but that he comes to the Most Merciful as a servant (ʿabdā)." This is very similar to what was said in Section [B'] when Allah 🙵 stated, "Lord of the heavens and the earth (as-samāwāti wal-arḍi) and whatever is between them - so worship Him (faʿbud-hu) and have patience for His worship (ʿibādati-hi)."

Finally, in the second from the last verse of the Sūrah, Allah 🙵 tells the Messenger 🙵 that He sent the Quran in their Arabic tongue to "give good news (litubashshira) thereby to the God-conscious." This ties back to the miracle given to Zakariyyā 🙵 when he was informed, "No doubt, We give you good news (nubashshiru-ka) of a boy named Yaḥyā." This may be a way for us to understand the type of reaction we should have when hearing the Quran. The elation of an old man being surprised with a righteous son should be the type of emotion the God-conscious feel when they learn of the forgiveness, pardon, grace, mercy, reward, and Paradise from Allah 🙵.

And with that we conclude our detailed dissection of the structure of Sūrah Maryam. Now we will look back at the macroscopic view of the Sūrah and analyze the themes and motifs running through the entirety of it.

Holistic Coherence of Sūrah Maryam

When we first began our observations of Sūrah Maryam, we proposed the following ring structure to the entire Sūrah:

A – Divine Intervention at Birth (2-40)
B – Ibrāhīm and His Father (41-50)
C' – Our Forefathers in Faith (51-58)
B' – Path to Salvation (59-65)
A' – Denying the True Reality (66-98)

Now that we have an appreciation of the content within each Section, we can better understand the connections between them.

Connections

- [A/A'] - The Sūrah begins with two stories of children being born with divine help. In each of those narratives there is a show of concern for the immediate future. Zakariyyā عليه السلام wants someone to inherit from him and carry on his legacy, while Maryam عليها السلام wants to avoid any negative aspersions against her honor. The corresponding section shows a complete lack of concern for the far future, that is, the Afterlife. The disbelievers are quoted again and again as having disregard for their next life, which leads to a lack of urgency in this life as well.
- The final section contains a passage that emphatically declares attributing a son to Allah ﷻ as a great blasphemy. This passage has the word, "son (walad)" repeated three times in quick succession. This usage of "son" may remind the audience of the only other usage of the word found outside of Section [A'], from the conclusion of Section [A], wherein Allah ﷻ appropriately states, "It is not appropriate for Allah to take any son (walad). He is perfect."
- [B/B'] - The story of Ibrāhīm عليه السلام and his father appears to be paired with the Section outlining the path to salvation. Just as Ibrāhīm عليه السلام gave his father irrefutable arguments and rationale for accepting Islam, Section [B'] clearly demonstrates the options one has when confronted with the choice between guidance and misguidance. Put another way, Section [B] tells us why we should accept guidance and Section [B'] tells us the outcome of that choice (or lack thereof).
- [C] - At the center of this wonderful Sūrah is the section about our forefathers in monotheism. Of particular note is the repeated usage of "prophet (nabiyy)" that is used throughout this passage. By men-

tioning so many prophets together, each with their own unique and miraculous story, it helps to drive home the point that ʿĪsā ﷺ is not a god. Recall that ʿĪsā ﷺ described himself the same way when he introduced himself to the world as a "prophet (nabiyy)."

Themes and Motifs

To conclude our study of Sūrah Maryam, we will take a brief look at how the contents of this Sūrah contribute to delivering a coherent message despite the seemingly numerous topics addressed. In particular, we will explore the motifs that have been running throughout the text and how they give further meaning to this already rich Sūrah.

1.

Family - The Sūrah presents a comprehensive view of family. There are narratives about childless parents, miraculous births, righteous children, disbelieving parents, upright brothers, and prophetic dynasties. Taken in totality, the Sūrah provides a detailed explanation of the prayer we are encouraged to say from Sūrah al-Furqān, "[And the servants of the Most Merciful are] those who say, 'Our Master, gift us from our spouses and children those who put our heart at ease, and make us leaders of the God-conscious.'" [28]

Another interesting point is brought up by Layla Alhassen who comments in her paper analyzing the first half of Sūrah Maryam that, "the sura begins with the themes of God and family, but the theme of family becomes less prominent and the theme of God and faith eventually replaces it. God, the narrator, who is initially central to the sura's depiction of family, eventually replaces the family completely."[29]

2.

Seclusion - Related to the motif of family is the theme of seclusion that we see repeated in many of the stories. Additionally, retreating into isolation typically resulted in being gifted or aided with family. Zakariyyā ﷺ prayed in private and was gifted Yaḥyā ﷺ. Maryam ﷺ put up a veil between her-

---

28 وَٱلَّذِينَ يَقُولُونَ رَبَّنَا هَبْ لَنَا مِنْ أَزْوَٰجِنَا وَذُرِّيَّٰتِنَا قُرَّةَ أَعْيُنٍ وَٱجْعَلْنَا لِلْمُتَّقِينَ إِمَامًا - 25:47

29 Alhassen, Leyla Ozgur, *A Structural Analysis of Sūrat Maryam, Verses 1-58*

self and others for worship and was gifted ʿĪsā ﵇. Ibrāhīm ﵇ left his father and community to be on his own and was gifted Isḥāq ﵇ and Yaʿqūb ﵇. Mūsā ﵇ met with Allah ﷻ for a one-on-one conversation and was aided with his brother, Hārūn ﵇. There are also other instances embedded in the back stories of the other prophets mentioned, but those aren't as explicit as the aforementioned examples.

3.

Love and Mercy (Raḥmah) - This was already mentioned as a theme in the introduction to this book. Building off of the author's points, Sūrah Maryam may be argued to be catered to a Christian audience with the frequent mention of Abrahamic prophets, and Maryam ﵇ and ʿĪsā ﵇ in particular. Christianity is also the religion most associated with preaching "love and mercy," so it is appropriate that Allah ﷻ would mention His name, the Most Merciful (ar-Raḥmān), or an Arabic derivative of "mercy (raḥmah)" sixteen times here. The mention of "the Most Merciful (ar-Raḥmān)" occurs sparingly in the beginning of the Sūrah and crescendos towards the concluding passages where the name recurs in almost every verse.

From a linguistic viewpoint, the usage of "mercy (raḥmah)" is doubly appropriate as it relates to family as well. The Arabic root letters for raḥmah are the same root letters in the word for "womb (raḥm)" which relates back to the other motifs mentioned above.

4.

Christ is Not Divine - Relating to all the aforementioned motifs, the argument for why ʿĪsā ﵇ is not divine is made subtly at first, but by the end of the Sūrah we have some of the most explicit statements mentioned in the Quran against any and all associations with Allah ﷻ.

It also seems as though most of the prophets mentioned in this Sūrah have some link to a divine intervention in their youth. Yaḥyā ﵇ was born to old and barren parents. ʿĪsā ﵇ was born to a virgin mother. Elsewhere in the Quran, Ibrāhīm ﵇ was saved from a burning fire.[30] Ismāʿīl ﵇ was saved

---

30 21:68-69 - قَالُوا حَرِّقُوهُ وَانصُرُوا آلِهَتَكُمْ إِن كُنتُمْ فَاعِلِينَ * قُلْنَا يَا نَارُ كُونِي بَرْدًا وَسَلَامًا عَلَىٰ إِبْرَاهِيمَ

from thirst and starvation in the Meccan desert.[31] Mūsā 🕮 was supposed to be killed as a baby, but miraculously survived by being floated down a river.[32] These all contribute to the argument that, despite 'Īsā 🕮 having a miraculous intervention in his life, he does not ascend to the level of "God," just like the other messengers and prophets who we given divine assistance.

Another subtle argument is the continued usage of "prophet (nabiyy)" that is used in almost every Section of this Sūrah. By linking all other prophets to being a "nabiyy," the listener should take note that 'Īsā 🕮 himself says, "No doubt, I am a servant of Allah. He gave me the Scripture and made me a prophet (nabiyyā)."

5.

Speech versus Silence[33] - One of the more subtle motifs has to do with the relationship between speech and silence. The Sūrah begins, "The mentioning (dhikru) of the mercy of your Lord to His servant, Zakariyyā." The Arabic root for dhikr, dha-ka-ra, has a relation of sound with the name Zakariyyā, whose name has the root letters za-ka-ra. Immediately after this seemingly play on words, the Sūrah says that his supplication was "silent (khafiyyā)." Next it is mentioned that the name Yaḥyā is so unique that no has had this name before, implying something which was never heard of. This is closely followed by a sign to Zakariyyā 🕮 of three days of silence.

After that comes the mention of Maryam 🕮 when she swore to be silent in front of her people, and suddenly the baby, who nobody expected to talk, began giving a sermon. Later in the Sūrah we're told that the inhabitants of Paradise will not hear "vain speech." There are more examples we will not list out, but it appears that this motif develops progressively through the Sūrah, reaching its culmination in the last verse.

In the final passage, Allah 🕮 says, "Indeed, We have made this [Quran] easy on your tongue to give good news to the God-conscious," and then the Sūrah ends with, "Do you perceive a single one of [the disbelievers] now, or hear as much as a whisper (rikzā)?" The word rikzā comes from the Arabic

---

31   14:37 - رَبَّنَا إِنِّى أَسْكَنتُ مِن ذُرِّيَّتِى بِوَادٍ غَيْرِ ذِى زَرْعٍ عِندَ بَيْتِكَ الْمُحَرَّمِ رَبَّنَا لِيُقِيمُوا الصَّلَاةَ فَاجْعَلْ أَفْئِدَةً مِّنَ النَّاسِ تَهْوِى إِلَيْهِمْ وَارْزُقْهُم مِّنَ الثَّمَرَاتِ لَعَلَّهُمْ يَشْكُرُونَ

32   28:7 - وَأَوْحَيْنَا إِلَى أُمِّ مُوسَى أَنْ أَرْضِعِيهِ فَإِذَا خِفْتِ عَلَيْهِ فَأَلْقِيهِ فِى الْيَمِّ وَلَا تَخَافِى وَلَا تَحْزَنِى إِنَّا رَادُّوهُ إِلَيْكِ وَجَاعِلُوهُ مِنَ الْمُرْسَلِينَ

33   Thank you Ammar Ljevaković for these incredible reflections

root, ra-ka-za, which are the same root letters Zakariyyā's name is derived from, but in reverse order. So, the Sūrah began contrasting speech and silence and ended contrasting speech and silence.

This motif would have been particularly powerful to the nascent Muslim community since this was revealed at a time when they were first beginning to preach openly about the religion. This very subtle theme may have acted as encouragement to preach the message publicly and confidently.

6.

Secrets[34] - Allah ﷻ being the One who knows all and who reveals what He wills is made very clear in this Sūrah through the many examples and narratives relayed throughout. Thus far, we have not mentioned the opening verse of the Sūrah, but now we can appreciate a rhetorical benefit of it. Allah ﷻ begins, "Kāf, Hā, Yā, ʿAyn, Ṣād." As the author explained earlier, Allah ﷻ alone knows the meanings of these letters. In other words, it is a sign signifying a secret of Allah ﷻ that is maintained. Also of note, this is the only verse in the Sūrah that does not have the same rhyme ending as the other verses. It sticks out phonetically as well as in meaning from the rest of the content.

Then, unlike the secret of Allah ﷻ which is never unveiled, Zakariyyā's intimate prayer is recorded in detail for all to hear. In contrast to this revealed secret, we move to a mystery that remains a mystery when an unnamed speaker communicates with Zakariyyā ﷺ. We are not told the speaker's identity, a narrative strategy which again serves to highlight Allah's ﷻ omniscience and our contrasting human lack of knowledge.[35] There are countless other examples in this beautiful Sūrah which all serve to highlight the stark contrast between Allah's infinite knowledge and our limited knowledge. Allah ﷻ reveals what He wants, when He wants, no matter how hidden or privileged the information may seem.

Conclusion

Hopefully we now have a better appreciation for the beauty, organiza-

---

34 The following is based on the work of Leyla Ozgur Alhassen in *A Structural Analysis of Sūrat Maryam, Verses 1-58*

35 Ibid. The identity of this speaker is revealed in Sūrah Āl ʿImrān, but the fact Allah ﷻ chose not to reveal that here may contribute to the message that's meant to be delivered in this Sūrah as opposed to another one.

tion, coherence, and genius of Allah's words. Nothing in His book is there by chance. Each word, each verse, and each passage are placed in a predetermined location that best suits the immediate context.

What we've also seen is that the parallels and structure of the Sūrah may act as a tool to help us better understand the Quran. The subtle meanings gleaned from the above analysis may lend itself to an additional method of "Tafsīr of the Quran by the Quran," which qualified scholars may utilize in future exegetical works.

This is far from a comprehensive view of the Sūrah's structure. There is much more documented that was either left out[36] or, more likely, not discovered yet. The Quran is a miracle that never ends, so our research of it is without end either. May Allah ﷻ accept this as a small contribution to better appreciating His words.

If the topic of the Quran's coherence interests you, please check out HeavenlyOrder.substack.com for a growing archive of examples from the Quran of organization and structure in many different verses and sūrahs.

Summary of All Structures

Here is a summarized graphic showing the multiple layers of structuring we uncovered in our study of this Sūrah:

36 The interested reader may see The Miraculous Birth Stories in the Interpretation of Sūrat Maryam (Q 19), An Exercise in a Discourse Grammar of the Qur'an by A.H Mathias Zahniser, Sūrat Maryam (Q. 19): Lexicon, Lexical Echoes, English Translation by Shawkat M. Toorawa and Sūrat Maryam (Q. 19): Comforting Muḥammad by M.A.S. Abdel Haleem.

<table>
<tr><th rowspan="2">MACRO STRUCTURE</th><th colspan="3">MICRO STRUCTURES</th></tr>
<tr><th>LEVEL 1</th><th>LEVEL 2</th><th>LEVEL 3</th></tr>
<tr><td rowspan="13">Ring (2-98)</td><td rowspan="5">Parallel (2-40)</td><td>Ring (2-11)</td><td></td></tr>
<tr><td>Ring (12-15)</td><td></td></tr>
<tr><td rowspan="2">Parallel (16-34a)</td><td>Ring (26-29)</td></tr>
<tr><td>Ring (30-34a)</td></tr>
<tr><td>Parallel (34b-40)</td><td></td></tr>
<tr><td rowspan="3">Ring (41-50)</td><td>Ring (41-46)</td><td>Parallel (42-45)</td></tr>
<tr><td>Parallel (47-49a)</td><td></td></tr>
<tr><td>Parallel (49b-50)</td><td></td></tr>
<tr><td>Ring (51-58)</td><td></td><td></td></tr>
<tr><td>Ring (59-65)</td><td></td><td></td></tr>
<tr><td rowspan="3">Ring (66-98)</td><td>Ring (66-74)</td><td rowspan="3"></td></tr>
<tr><td>Ring (75-82)</td></tr>
<tr><td>Ring (83-98)</td></tr>
</table>

BIBLIOGRAPHY

al-Ālūsī, Maḥmūd ibn ʿAbd Allah. *Rūh al-Maʿānī fī Tafsīr al-Quran al-ʿAẓīm wa al-Sabʿ al-Mathānī*. Beirut: Mu'assasah al-Risālah, 2010

al-Baghawī, al-Ḥussain ibn Masʿūd. *Maʿālim al-Tanzīl*. Saudi Arabia: Dār al-Ṭayyibah, 2010

al-Gharnāṭī, Muḥammad ibn Yūsuf. *al-Baḥr al-Muḥīṭ fī al-Tafsīr*. Makkah: al-Maktabah al-Tijāriyyah

al-Maẓharī, Muḥammad Thanā Allah. *al-Tafsīr al-Maẓharī*. Beirut: Dār al-Kutub al-ʿIlmiyyah, 2007

al-Qurṭubī, Muḥammad ibn Aḥmad. *al-Jāmiʿ lī Aḥkām al-Quran*. Damascus: Mu'assasah al-Risālah, 2013

al-Rāzī, Fakhr al-Dīn. *Mafātīḥ al-Ghayb*. Cairo: Dār al-Ḥadīth, 2012

al-Shawkānī, Muḥammad ibn ʿAlī. *Fatḥ al-Qadīr*. Beirut: Dār ibn Ḥazm, 2005

al-Ṭabarī, Muḥammad ibn Jarīr. *Jāmiʿ al-Bayān ʿan Ta'wīl Āyy al-Quran*. Beirut: Dār ibn Ḥazm, 2013

al-Zūḥailī, Wahbah. *al-Tafsīr al-Munīr fī al-ʿAqīdah wa al-Sharīʿah wa al-Manhaj*. Damascus: Dār al-Fikr, 2009

ibn ʿĀshūr, Muḥammad al-Ṭāhir. *Tafsīr al-Taḥrīr wa al-Tanwīr*. Beirut:

Mu'assasah al-Tārīkh

Ibn Kathīr, Ismāʿīl. *Tafsīr al-Quran al-ʿAẓīm*. Saudi Arabia: Dār ʿĀlam al-Kutub, 2004

Quṭb, Syed. *fī Ẓilāl al-Quran*. Cairo: Dār al-Shurūq, 2009

Shafi, Muhammad. *Maʿriful Qur'an*. Pakistan: Maktaba-e-Darul-Uloom, 2003

ABOUT THE AUTHOR

Shaykh Furhan Zubairi was born in 1983 in Indianapolis, IN. Shortly thereafter, he moved and spent most of his youth in Southern California, graduating from high school in Irvine in 2001. He began his pursuit of Islamic knowledge and spirituality at the Institute of Knowledge (IOK) in 1998 where he started the memorization of the Quran and studied the primary books in the Islamic sciences and Arabic language. After starting college, he took a break and went to Karachi, Pakistan for 9 months to complete the memorization of the Quran at Jamiʿah Binoria. He returned home and completed his B.S. in Biological Sciences from the University of California, Irvine in 2005. He then traveled to Egypt to further his studies of the Arabic language. Thereafter, his pursuit of Islamic knowledge led him back to Pakistan where he completed a formal 'Alamiyyah degree (Masters in Arabic and Islamic Studies) at the famous Jami'ah Darul-Uloom in Karachi, where he studied with prominent scholars. He has obtained numerous ijaazaat (traditional licenses) in the six authentic books of hadith Siha Sittah as well as the Muwattas of Imam Malik and Imam Muhammad and has also received certification in the field of Islamic Finance. Shaykh Furhan Zubairi serves as the Dean of the Seminary Program (IOKseminary.com) at the Institute of Knowledge in Diamond Bar, CA. He regularly delivers khutbahs and lectures at various Islamic Centers and events in Southern California.

The Institute of Knowledge Seminary Curriculum Series is a collection of books designed to build literacy amongst the Muslim community in the major branches of Islamic Studies including ʿAqīdah, Quran, Ḥadīth, Fiqh, Uṣūl al-Fiqh, Sīrah and Tazkiyah. The books go hand in hand with the courses offered through the IOK Seminary Program, which provides educational courses, programs and seminars to the wider local and international community.

Visit **IOKseminary.com** to learn more, view the full catalog and attend classes on-site, online and on-demand.

OTHER AVAILABLE WORKS:

- An Introduction to the Sciences of the Qur'an
- Introduction to Ḥadīth Studies
- Introduction to Uṣūl al-Fiqh
- Hajj and Umrah: A Brief Guide
- In the Company of Scholars: A Commentary on al-Nawawi's Forty Hadith
- In the Company of the Quran: An Explanation of Sūrah al-Kahf

FORTHCOMING WORKS:

- A Brief Introduction to Tajwīd
- Tafsīr of Juz ʿAmma
- An Introduction to the Ḥanafī Madhab

Printed in Great Britain
by Amazon

38270127R00135